"Stephen Olford has  ing beautiful expository ︴ ︴ ︴her of preachers. The Step︴ ︴ ︴. Olford Biblical Preaching Library provides substantive examples on how to do it. It will be a great help to many preachers."

Dr. R. Kent Hughes, Senior Pastor
College Church, Wheaton, Illinois

"Stephen Olford is a master expositor and genius at outline clarity. . . . Most preachers can neither walk across the street or travel across the continent to hear him. But they can glean the treasures of his preaching life from The Stephen F. Olford Biblical Preaching Library. I heartily commend this resource."

Dr. Maxie E. Dunham, Senior Pastor
Christ United Methodist Church, Memphis, Tennessee

"Every informed preacher of the Word of God knows of the spiritual power, impeccable scholarship, and practicality of the materials produced by Stephen Olford. Without reservation, I commend The Stephen F. Olford Biblical Preaching Library."

Dr. Adrian Rogers, Senior Pastor
Bellevue Baptist Church, Cordova, Tennessee

Books in the Stephen F. Olford Biblical Preaching Library

Biblical Answers to Personal Problems
Committed to Christ and His Church
Fresh Lessons from Former Leaders
The Pulpit and the Christian Calendar 1
The Pulpit and the Christian Calendar 2
The Pulpit and the Christian Calendar 3
Believing Our Beliefs
Living Words and Loving Deeds

The Pulpit and the Christian Calendar 3

Stephen F. Olford

BAKER BOOK HOUSE
Grand Rapids, Michigan 49516

Copyright © 1992 by
Baker Book House Company
P.O. Box 6287, Grand Rapids, MI 49516-6287

ISBN: 0-8010-6723-5

Second printing, April 1993

Printed in the United States of America

These resources were adapted from material published by the Institute for Biblical Preaching, Box 757800, Memphis, TN 38175-7800.

The New King James Version is used as the basis for this study. Also used is the King James Version (kjv).

The author is grateful to the many copyright owners for the use of their material.

Contents

Introduction   7

Part 1: Annual Occasions

1. New Year's Sunday: *Henceforth unto Him*
   (2 Corinthians 5:14–21)   11
2. New Year's Sunday: *A Milestone in the Ministry*
   (Acts 28:11–16)   20
3. New Year's Sunday: *The Companionship of Christ*
   (Exodus 33:12–23; Joshua 1:1–9)   29
4. Palm Sunday: *Behold Your King*
   (Matthew 21:1-11)   38
5. Easter Sunday: *The Gospel of the Resurrection*
   (1 Corinthians 15:1–20)   45
6. Labor Day Sunday: *Spiritual Stewardship*
   (1 Peter 4:7-11)   53
7. Thanksgiving Sunday: *The Duty of Thankfulness*
   (Psalm 92:1–15)   62

Part 2: Special Occasions

8. Baptism Service: *The Blessing of Obedience*
   (Matthew 3:13–17; Luke 3:21–22;
   John 1:29–34)   73

9. Missions Sunday: *The Whole Word to the Whole World* (Mark 16:14–20) 82
10. Youth Sunday: *The Mind of Youth* (Ecclesiastes 11:9–12:7) 92
11. Youth Sunday: *The Way of Youth* (Psalm 119:9) 100
12. Youth Sunday: *The Yoke of Youth* (Lamentations 3:22–33) 108
13. Youth Sunday: *The Gift of Youth* (John 6:5–14) 117
14. Youth Sunday: *The Role of Youth* (1 Timothy 4:10–16) 124

Endnotes 135
For Further Reading 138

Introduction

This is a companion to *The Pulpit and the Christian Calendar 1* and *2*. The only difference is that here we are dealing with annual occasions as well as special occasions. The annual occasions all represent important and memorable days in the course of a calendar year. I know that the celebration of such "holy days" was a cause for intolerance and difference of opinion on the part of some in the early church (see Rom. 14:1–12). But in that context Paul argues that, whether or not we observe these annual occasions, we must respect the conscience of others for the Lord's sake. We stand or fall to our own master, for "we are the Lord's" (v. 8).

Having made that observation, I must remind preachers, teachers, and evangelists that special occasions are wonderful oportunities for evangelism and church outreach. In my many years of ministry, both in pastorates and "on the road," I have addressed more people at New Year's, Easter sunrise, and Thanksgiving services than at any other given time (with the exception of the concluding days of citywide crusades or conventions). Paul's God-given philosophy was, "I have become all things to all men, that I might by all means save some" (1 Cor. 9:22). We must perform in like manner.

The special occasions speak for themselves. A baptismal service was—and is—a holy event, as far as I am concerned. Indeed, I planned this occasion with great care and prayer. It usually took place on the last Sunday of the month and provided an opportunity to challenge my congregation to declare their faith in discipleship and dedication.

Mission Sunday was a call to "go," "give," and "pray" for worldwide evangelization. During crusades I always made Friday night "mission night." There are thousands of missionaries all over the world that can point to this "special occasion."

Then it goes without saying that "youth Sundays" are priority number one! The preacher was right when he wrote, "Remember now your Creator in the days of your youth, before the difficult days come, and the years draw near when you say, 'I have no pleasure in them'" (Eccles. 12:1).

It is fitting and proper, therefore, that we should maximize the days of the Christian calendar as we "preach the word" in season and "do the work of an evangelist" (2 Tim. 4:2, 5).

Stephen F. Olford

Part 1

Annual Occasions

1

New Year's Sunday: *Henceforth unto Him*
2 Corinthians 5:14–21

"For the love of Christ constrains us, because . . . if One died for all, then all died; and He died for all, that those who live should no longer live for themselves, but for Him who died for them and rose again" (5:14–15).

Introduction

What a text for a new year! When Paul wrote these words he was thinking back to that moment in his life when old things passed away and all things became new. This experience was so revolutionary that he employs unusual language to describe this spiritual transformation. As we study the context we discover that the expression "Henceforth unto Him" implies:

I. The Termination of the Self-Life

"For the love of Christ constrains us, because we judge thus: that if One died for all, then all died; and He died for all, that those who live should live no longer for themselves, but for Him who died for them and rose again" (5:14–15). The meaning of that word "constrains" is both powerful and precious. The Greek denotes the thought of being "confined within the limits of a certain course of action which never deviates from one set purpose." This is how the love of God motivated and actuated the Lord Jesus. He could say, "I have a baptism to be baptized with; and how am I *straitened* till it be accomplished!" (Luke 12:50 KJV). This is our word. For him, it meant the path of the cross, even unto death, that he might be raised to the glory of God the Father.

In like manner, this is how Paul interprets this word. Compelled and impelled by the love of Christ, there had to be:

A. *The Extinguishing of the Old Self*

He says, "we judge thus: that if One died for all, then all died" (5:14). When Paul viewed Calvary he saw Christ not only representing his sin, but also his old self-life. This is why he could say, "I have been crucified with Christ" (Gal. 2:20).

This is one of the greatest discoveries we can make. When Jesus died at Calvary he not only died for us, but we died with him. This means the termination of the self-life. Any attempt on our part to return to that life is a repudiation of our union with Christ in death. Indeed, it is an insult to the very Christ who died that we might be saved from our old corrupt nature.

Illustration

When an immigrant comes to America, before he can become a citizen he must renounce all his commitments and allegiance to his former homeland and pledge 100 percent allegiance to America. Then and only then will the U.S. government grant him citizenship. That's the way it is with Jesus. When you accept Christ as Savior and Lord you renounce sin, self, and Satan completely. You can't "split time" by serving Satan part-time and Christ part-time.[1]

B. The Relinquishing of the New Self

"And he died for all, that those who live should live no longer for themselves, but for Him who died for them and rose again" (5:15). When Paul declares "I have been crucified with Christ" he does not end it there but goes on to say, "it is no longer I who live, but *Christ lives in me;* and the life which I now live in the flesh I live by faith in the Son of God, who loved me and gave Himself for me" (Gal. 2:20). While the old self—which represented his past life—was extinguished at Calvary, the new self—which represented his redeemed personality—had to be yielded to Christ in order to complete his response to the constraining love of Christ.

Even though we have been crucified with Christ we still possess our individual personalities. Calvary does not obliterate the real "you" and "me." Now that we have been delivered from our old selves, the question arises as to what we are going to do with our new selves. Paul gives the answer in the passage before us. He says, "Those who live should live no longer for themselves, but for Him who died for them and rose again" (5:15); in other words, *Henceforth unto Him.* We cannot kneel before the cross and recognize the wonder of the self-giving of the Lord Jesus without exclaiming:

> Love so amazing, so divine,
> Demands my soul, my life, my all.

John Calvin, the great theologian and reformer, came to this point in his life when he looked into the face of his master and cried, "Lord, I give thee everything; I keep back nothing for myself." "Relinquishing implies a giving up of something desirable and connotes compulsion or force of necessity."[2]

II. The Introduction of the Faith-Life

"Therefore, from now on, we regard no one according to the flesh. Even though we have known Christ according to the flesh, yet now we know Him thus no longer. Therefore, if anyone is in Christ, he is a new creation; old things have passed away; behold, all things have become new" (5:16–17). Paul shows in these two verses how his determination to live for Christ, rather than self, found expression in a faith-life. The judgment he had formed concerning the death and resurrection of Christ had effected such a transformation in his outlook that his view of man had totally changed.

Paul's experience can take place in our lives, for in these words of the apostle we learn that:

A. *The Faith-Life Accepts a New Conception of Man*

"Therefore, from now on, we regard no one according to the flesh" (5:16). To be united to Christ through his death and resurrection is to gain new standards of judgment and new ways of looking at things. Paul had ceased to judge men by outward appearances and circumstances of life, such as color, wealth, rank, culture, or knowledge. The one question that mattered to him was whether man, by his own act and choice, had become a new creation through the death and resurrection of Christ.

To strengthen his argument, Paul affirmed that even his judgment of *Christ* had been totally altered by his understanding of what had happened at Calvary. Before, Jesus was nothing more to Paul than a man who was born in obscurity, lived in restricted surroundings, and died a humiliating death; in fact, because of this evaluation of Jesus, he dismissed him as an imposter and persecuted his followers. But after Saul's conversion on the Damascus road, all was changed. Jesus was now the Redeemer of all men for "He [had] died for *all*" (5:15). From now on all men were equal—irrespective of color, class, or creed. Without distinction, all men needed a Savior; therefore, all men must be included in his redemptive concern.

B. The Faith-Life Accepts a New Creation of Man

"Therefore, if anyone is in Christ, he is a new creation; old things have passed away; behold, all things have become new" (5:17). Here the apostle reaches a climax. The regenerating experience that had taken place in his life could take place in others. God had prophesied through his servant, Isaiah, that a day would dawn when men and women would become new creations in Christ Jesus. Isaiah 43:18–19, 21 reads: "Do not remember the former things, nor consider the things of old. Behold, I will do a new thing.... This people I have formed for Myself; they shall declare My praise." So in the words of Professor R. V. G. Tasker it is true to say: "Each man regenerated by the Spirit of God is a new creation, and a world in which such new creations exist is potentially at least a new world."[3] In this new world there are no personal discriminations or racial tensions, for we are "all one in Christ Jesus" (Gal. 3:28). No thoughtful man or woman can understand this truth in our contemporary world and not be persuaded by the relevance and validity of our gospel. This is the essence of our Christian faith—a faith that accepts a new conception of man and a new creation of man because Jesus Christ has made all things new.

Illustration

In the Salvation Army, and in every place where he was known, Commissioner Samuel Logan Brengle was loved. No name is more revered among Salvationists than his, for there has been no soldier more saintly nor officer more spiritually effective than this quiet-spoken prophet of God. His biographer, Clarence W. Hall relates that shortly after Brengle had had a deep experience of God he "walked out over Boston Commons . . . weeping for joy and praising God . . . I was filled with love for all his creatures. I heard the little sparrows chattering; I loved them. I saw a little worm wriggling across my path; I stepped over it; I didn't want to hurt any living thing. I loved the dogs, I loved the horses, I loved the little urchins on the street, I loved the strangers who hurried past me, I loved the heathen—I loved the whole world!"[4]

III. The Operation of the Christ-Life

"All things are of God who has reconciled us to Himself through Jesus Christ, and has given us the ministry of reconciliation" (5:18; see also vv. 19–21). When a person has experienced the termination of the self-life and the introduction of the faith-life, Christ becomes central in all his actions and conduct. The phrase that sums up the supreme operation of any Christian is what Paul terms here "the ministry of reconciliation" (5:18). This is the purpose for which the Lord Jesus came into the world. From the cradle to the cross, and from the cross to the crown, he was (and is) concerned with one great operation: *reconciliation.* Very simply, this involves two things:

A. There Is a World to Reach

"God was in Christ reconciling the world to Himself, not imputing their trespasses to them, and has committed to us the word of reconciliation" (5:19). Here are words which cause us to pause in "wonder, love, and praise." No one can finally interpret them since they relate to "the ultimate paradox of the atonement." We just have to believe that when the Lord Jesus hung upon that cross "God was in Christ reconciling the world to Himself" (5:19). For this to happen, the Lord Jesus, who knew no sin, had to be made sin for us "that we might become the righteousness of God in Him" (5:21). From the divine perspective, God did everything to break down the enmity and hostility of sin which separated man from God. But you and I also play a role in this ministry of reconciliation. Our task is to reach a world that has been reconciled to God through the death of his Son. This is the meaning of the Great Commission when Jesus said, "All authority has been given to Me in heaven and on earth. Go therefore and make disciples of all the nations, baptizing them in the name of the Father and of the Son and of the Holy Spirit, teaching them to observe all things that I have commanded you; and lo, I am with you always, even to the end of the age" (Matt. 28:18–20). No one can claim to know a Christ-centered life without a passion to reach the world with "the ministry of reconciliation" (5:18).

Illustration

When the noble Bruce, hero of Bannockburn, died, his heart was extracted and encased in a silver casket by Black Douglas and carried with the army. Douglas died fighting the Moors. Before he fell he threw the heart of Bruce into the thickest of the fray and urged his soldiers to follow that heart and conquer. Christ's heart is in the densest of heathenism, and Christians must have their hearts there if they would feel his heartthrob.[5]

B. There Is a Word to Preach

"God . . . has committed to us the *word* of reconciliation. Therefore we are ambassadors for Christ, as though God were pleading through us: we implore you on Christ's behalf, be reconciled to God" (5:19–20). We have a message that is distinctive and dynamic. Paul was so convinced of this that he could face the proud metropolis of Rome and affirm: "I am not ashamed of the gospel of Christ, for it is the power of God to salvation for everyone who believes, for the Jew first and also for the Greek" (Rom. 1:16). It is the message of a Savior who died, who lives and reigns to change men, to change society, and to change the world. One day this gospel is going to effect a universal transformation; but, in the meantime, it is God's purpose to effect individual transformations. God always starts from center to circumference. It was Samuel Zwemer who said, "The man who goes out to change society is an optimist, but the man who goes out to change society without changing the individual is a lunatic!"

Illustration

When Martin Luther returned to Wittenberg in later years and was greeted as the "Hero of Worms," he said: "Our first object must be to win men's hearts; and for that purpose we must preach the gospel. Today the Word will fall into one heart, tomorrow into another, and it will operate to such a purpose as it was sent. God does more by His Word alone than you and I and all the world by our united strength. God lays hold upon the heart; and when the heart is taken, all is won."[6]

We have been constituted ambassadors to entreat men in Christ's stead to be reconciled to God. As Professor Tasker reminds us: "An ambassador is a title both proud and humble." This is highly significant because, as ambassadors for Christ, we must be characterized by divine authority and humility when we preach the Word. An ambassador is not a man who communicates his own opinions or speculations, but speaks with the authority and name of his government. We have nothing for which to apologize. Our message comes from God himself, and so with apostolic boldness we are to preach the Word with confidence and courage, yet with divine humility. We are told that ambassadors are usually chosen for their dignity and diplomacy; therefore, we must plead with men "by the meekness and gentleness of Christ" (2 Cor. 10:1). These two qualities are the distinctives which are lacking in our preaching today. It is bad enough to lack the authority of Christ, but even worse to fall short of the humility of Christ. Can we imagine anything more compelling and persuasive than to allow God, through us, to beseech men and women, in Christ's stead, to be reconciled? This is the highest concept of service in a world fast hurrying to destruction. This is the operation of the Christ-life, and no one can know a Christ-centered life without this burden to reach the world and to preach the Word.

Conclusion

We have seen, then, what is meant by our motto for the year, "Henceforth unto Him." It implies the termination of the self-life, it invites the introduction of the faith-life, and it involves the operation of the Christ-life. What a motto to motivate our living and serving in this coming year! May God grant us, each one, to say and to live from this moment and forever "Henceforth unto Him."

New Year's Sunday: *A Milestone in the Ministry*
Acts 28:11–16

"When Paul saw . . . [the brethren], he thanked God and took courage" (28:15).

Introduction

Paul had reached a milestone in his ministry. After years of thinking, praying, writing, traveling, and suffering, he had arrived at Rome. To him, this was the fulfillment of a God-given dream. While his arrival on the outskirts of the great metropolis was not as he had originally envisaged (he was a prisoner and close to exhaustion in spirit, soul, and body) "he thanked God and took courage" (28:15).

We all reach milestones in our ministries for God, but do we ever stop to thank God and take courage? Here is a divine principle which should govern all Christian living. Every day we should thank God and take courage, but particularly when he brings to pass the fulfillment of some heaven-given dream, vision, or long-expected event.

Let us examine our text and look for the secret that made Paul thank God and take courage. Quite clearly, his thankfulness had to do with:

I. A Backward Look

"When Paul saw them, he thanked God" (28:15). The apostle's cause of thankfulness had a deeper significance than the spontaneous and immediate joy of meeting the brethren from Rome, he was deeply thankful because the arrival of those brethren represented:

A. The Fulfillment of a Repeated Prayer

"He thanked God" (28:15). About five years previously he had written an epistle to the believers at Rome in which he had said: "God is my witness, whom I serve with my spirit in the gospel of His Son, that without ceasing I make mention of you *always* in my prayers, making request if, by some means, now at last I may find a way in the will of God to come to you" (Rom. 1:9–10). Then he concluded his letter with an earnest request for traveling mercies and the fullness of the blessing of the gospel of Christ. He wrote: "I know that when I come to you, I shall come in the fullness of the blessing of the gospel of Christ. Now I beg you, brethren, through the Lord Jesus Christ, and through the love of the Spirit, that you strive together with me in your prayers to God for me, that I may be delivered from those in Judea who do not believe . . . that I may come to you" (Rom. 15:29–32).

What transpired throughout the intervening years fills nearly two-thirds of the Book of the Acts. True, mighty exploits were done for God, but not without facing death again and again. There were stonings, beatings, imprisonments, a shipwreck, a snake bite, and, many believe, recurring malarial fever. Is it any wonder that when Paul saw the brethren from Rome he gave thanks? God had answered prayer and Paul was satisfied.

Have you reached a milestone in your spiritual experience? Have you paused to thank God for answered prayer? It may be that the answer has not come in the way you expected. Indeed, you may have to look back on trials, suffering, and even sickness unto death, but God has brought you through. Will you not thank God and take courage?

B. The Fulfillment of a Restated Promise

"He thanked God" (28:15). Twice the Lord appeared to Paul and assured him he would reach Rome. The first time was in a Roman castle in Jerusalem, after he had almost been lynched (see Acts 23:11). The second instance was on a storm-tossed ship when, humanly speaking, all hope of being saved was gone (see Acts 27:24). The apostle had not forgotten these restated promises; he could rejoice and give thanks at their fulfillment.

Have you thanked God for all the revelations, blessings, and promises he has given you throughout your lifetime?

C. The Fulfillment of a Revealed Purpose

"He thanked God" (28:15). No one can read through Romans without being confronted with the revealed purpose of God for Christian living. Paul writes of being "called according to His purpose" and being "conformed to the image of his Son" (Rom. 8:28–29).

The question arises as to whether these great truths had affected the lives of the believers in Rome. One look at these brethren and Paul thanked God, and took courage (28:15). Their presence indicated far more to the apostle than appears on the surface.

Scholars tell us that the Greek significance for the

phrase "they came to *meet* us" is that of a city deputation going out to meet a general, a king, or a conqueror. Some believers had traveled 43 miles to the Appii Forum; others 33 miles to the Three Inns, to welcome an emaciated prisoner in chains as a world-famous celebrity! They were unafraid of being identified with a preacher under arrest! Here was growth and grace in Christ, and Paul saw it, thanked God, and took courage.

Illustration
Many people have become successful in spite of adverse circumstances. Nathaniel Hawthorne lost his position in the customhouse at Salem, Massachusetts. Dismayed, he told his wife the unfortunate news, expecting her to be upset. To his surprise, she was delighted: "Now you can continue work on your book." With her encouragement, he finished *The Scarlet Letter*—according to critics, one of the finest novels ever written in the United States. Take courage and thank God that his purpose is being fulfilled.[1]

II. A Forward Look

"When Paul saw . . . he . . . took courage" (28:15). The word *courage* means *good cheer, boldness,* and *confidence.* It is a Christian quality that enables a man to endure suffering and accomplish arduous achievements. It is that touch from heaven which carries a person beyond the attainments of normal habits or selfish interests. It is the strong and silent characteristic of godliness which never vaunts itself. And so "Paul . . . took courage" (28:15), and that in a twofold respect:

A. He Sensed Courage Through the Fellowship of the Saints

"When Paul saw . . . [the brethren], he . . . took courage" (28:15). We have already noted the welcome that these brethren accorded Paul, receiving him as a general, a king, and a conqueror. Their lives had been transformed by his ministry of pen and prayer, and they wanted him to know it.

And he needed such encouragement. The apostle appears to have been in a mood of discouragement at this time. For one thing, he was recovering from the rigors of travel sickness and weakness. More important was the apprehension of all that lay ahead. This was *the* crisis of his great career. He was too knowledgeable not to be aware of the pressures of a great city, the cruel suffering of imprisonment, but, above all, the solemn responsibility of conquering Rome with the gospel. A deep sense of loneliness concerning the ministry threatened to overwhelm him, had not the saints come out to *meet* him. And when Paul saw them he took courage.

How many a missionary, a Christian businessman, a preacher under unspeakable strain, has collapsed altogether because there were no brethren to meet him and encourage him in the Lord.

Illustration

The story is told of a fireman who was trying to reach a poor woman who was crying for help at the window of a burning house. One among the crowd below cried, "You can't do it, come down." The fireman was already badly burned and almost choked by smoke. He began to descend, leaving the woman to her fate, when a man shouted, "Give him a cheer!" The crowd that had gathered made the air ring with their encouragement, whereupon the fireman stopped, and again ascended toward the window, and aided by the cheers of the multitude brought the woman to safety. Ask yourself: Are you a cheerleader or a cheer-killer?

Illustration

In enforcing the duty of the congregation to encourage their minister, the famous Dr. R. W. Dale of Birmingham, England once said: "There are times when the most buoyant sink into despondency, when a great, chilly mist creeps over the soul of those who have the largest happiness in the service of God, and they feel as if their strength is gone. Not very long ago, one of these evil moods was upon me, but as I was passing along one of the streets of Birmingham, a poor but decently dressed woman, laden with parcels, stopped me and said, 'God bless you, Dr. Dale!' Her face was unknown to me, so I thanked her and asked her name. 'Never mind my name,' was her answer, 'but if only you knew what you have done in my life and what a happy home you have given me! God bless you, Dr. Dale.' 'That moment,' adds Dr. Dale, 'the mist broke, the sunlight came, and I breathed again the free air of the mountains of God.'"

B. He Sought Courage from the Fountainhead of the Spirit

"He . . . took courage" (28:15). Wonderful as is the encouragement of the saints, it will never take the place of the fullness of the Spirit.

For Paul, this moment was a milestone in his ministry. If ever he needed Holy Spirit-boldness and courage it was now. As he landed at Rome's port named Puteoli he could see, to the north, the fleets of Roman warships. Nearby were the crowded beaches and colored sails of the yachts of the wealthy citizens. Then there was Puteoli itself with its wharfs, stone houses, and granaries. Here was Rome with all its power, pomp, and splendor, yet here was Rome with all its sin, vice, and wickedness. But above all, here was Rome with its needy multitudes and missionary challenge. Paul had spent months thinking through the events that awaited him, and he knew that only heaven-sent courage would enable him to be:

1. A Preacher for God in Rome

"He . . . took courage" (28:15). Five years previously he had written: "So, as much as is in me, I am ready to preach the gospel to you who are in Rome also. For I am not ashamed of the gospel of Christ, for it is the power of God to salvation for everyone who believes, for the Jew first and also for the Greek. For in it the righteousness of God is revealed from faith to faith; as it is written, 'The just shall live by faith'" (Rom. 1:15–17). Three missionary journeys had taught Paul that only Holy Spirit courage could enable a man to stand by the truth when all the forces of hell were against him.

If ever we needed this quality of courage it is today. In the most subtle and yet relentless manner, the enemy is gaining ground—not only in the world at large, but in the church of Christ. The authority of the Bible, the deity of Christ, and the efficacy of the cross, not to speak of other doctrines of our faith, are being attacked. We are being told that it is old-fashioned to preach the simple gospel. Therefore, moral standards are being relaxed, and the authority of the ministry is being challenged on every hand. Only those with holy courage will ever survive the onslaughts of Satan. So *take* courage. Take it by faith. Take it in the person of the Holy Spirit.

Paul further knew that he needed such courage to be:

2. A Prisoner for God in Rome

"He . . . took courage" (28:15). In a few months' time we find Paul calling himself "a prisoner of Christ Jesus" (Philem. 1:1). Instead of succumbing to his circumstances, he made them the very platform for the extension of his ministry. The church at Philippi had written to him expressing its concern regarding his imprisonment, but this courageous man had replied, "I want you to know . . . that the things which happened to me have actually turned out for the furtherance of the gospel, so that it has become evident to the whole palace guard . . . that my chains are in Christ" (Phil. 1:12–13). Soldier after soldier, chained to his side, had been led to a saving knowledge of Christ, so that the palace of Caesar was feeling the impact of this man's ministry! Indeed, Rome was being slowly but surely conquered for Jesus. What a challenge this is to us!

Illustration

Determination to maintain a positive attitude about our circumstances makes the difference between success and failure. Winston Churchill failed twice to achieve an elected office during the early 1920s and had little political influence throughout the 1930s. But he kept developing his talents, and in 1940 he became the Prime Minister of England. Today he is acclaimed as a great hero. Paul had planned to go to Rome as a free man but was taken there as a prisoner instead. Nevertheless, Paul turned what could have been failure into advancement for the cause of Christ.[2]

3. A PENMAN FOR GOD IN ROME

"He . . . took courage" (28:15). Addressing the saints at Philippi, Paul says, "To write the same thing to you is not tedious, but for you it is safe" (Phil. 3:1). Many argue from this verse that Paul had already written letters to this church as to many other assemblies. In other words, Paul had found a real ministry in using his pen for God. As you are probably aware, the apostle wrote six epistles before his imprisonment, but no fewer than seven during his two periods in Rome—although some maintain that two of the seven may have been written in Macedonia during his temporary release in A.D. 63–67. What is important, however, is that those years of incarceration produced such creative and instructive teaching as is found in Ephesians and Colossians. As Dr. Graham Scroggie says, "No one can read the Prison Epistles without feeling that they have in them an element which is wanting, for the most part, in the previous group."

What a blow this strikes at the pessimistic defeatism of so much of our church life! We are forever talking about what we cannot do because of lack of funds, or space, or personnel. But here is a man who took courage, even in the restricted confines of a prison, and through his pen reached a world! God often shuts us up to situations in order to prove him in far more effective ways of service and blessing. All we need is disciplined faith to thank God and take courage.

Conclusion

We have looked at a milestone in a man's ministry. The backward look should teach us how to thank God for all things. The forward look should instruct us how to take courage and go forward, regardless of the scorn of the world, the weakness of the flesh, or the fury of the devil. We are on God's side and he has a glorious purpose to fulfill in every one of our lives. Let us, then, accept this milestone in our ministry and thank God, take courage, and go forward.

New Year's Sunday: *The Companionship of Christ*
Exodus 33:12–23; Joshua 1:1–9

"He Himself said, 'I will never leave you nor forsake you.' So we may boldly say:'The LORD is my helper; I will not fear. What can man do to me?'" (Heb. 13:5–6).

Introduction

If you were to ask why I am facing the New Year with optimism, confidence, and joy it is because God has given this promise: "I will never leave you nor forsake you" (Heb. 13:5). Whatever the next twelve months may hold—uncertainty, perplexity, bewilderment, defeat, or victory—one thing is sure: the companionship of Christ every step of the way.

Consider three glorious thoughts that emerge from a knowledge of the Lord's abiding presence:

I. A Life of Contentment

"Be content with such things as you have" (Heb. 13:5). The curse of our modern age is covetousness, greed, discontent, and a sense of frustration. It is a disease, a canker, eating away at the vitals of men and women throughout our land, leaving them dissatisfied, disillusioned, and discontented. The only antidote is knowing Jesus Christ as our constant companion and friend. In him is:

A. The Source of Contentment

"Be content. . . . For He Himself has said, 'I will never leave you nor forsake you'" (Heb. 13:5). God has made all things available to us through the cross of his Son, for example, "He who did not spare His own Son, but delivered him up for us all, how shall He not with Him also freely give us all things?" (Rom. 8:32); "the living God . . . gives us richly all things to enjoy" (1 Tim. 6:17); and again: "whether . . . things present or things to come—all are yours. And you are Christ's, and Christ is God's" (1 Cor. 3:22–23). Everything that is in God is in Christ, and everything that is in Christ is for me! Because I know his abiding, indwelling presence I am content, for he is the source of all contentment.

Illustration

We often quote the verse from the 23rd Psalm: "The Lord is my shepherd; I shall not want" (v. 1). A little girl was asked to recite it at an anniversary service. She tried hard but could not remember the words. Then she blurted out, "The Lord is my shepherd, that's all I want!"—and she was right. Truly, everything is in Jesus and we are complete in him. He is our source of contentment.

B. The Spirit of Contentment

"Having food and clothing . . . be content" for "godliness with contentment is great gain" (1 Tim. 6:8, 6). With these words Paul warned Timothy to watch those who tried to be rich. Such would "fall into temptation and a snare, and into many foolish and harmful lusts which drown men in destruction and perdition. For the love of money is a root of all kinds of evil" (1 Tim. 6:9–10).

There is greed, jealousy, strife, and frustration in the world today because of deep-seated covetousness—one of the characteristics of man's sinful nature.

But the state of the Christian is one of contentment. Paul affirmed, "I have learned in whatever state I am, to be content." He discovered the secret of how to abound, how to be abased, how to be full, and how to be empty. He learned by experience that with Jesus Christ living within he could "do all things through Christ" who strengthened him (Phil. 4:13). Wherever you look in Scripture it speaks of the contentment of the overflowing life.

1. Physical Contentment

David says, "I have been young, and now am old; yet I have not seen the righteous forsaken, nor his descendants begging bread" (Ps. 37:25). In his Sermon on the Mount, the master exhorts us to "seek first the kingdom of God and His righteousness, and all these things shall be added to you" (Matt. 6:33).

2. Spiritual Contentment

"Blessed are those who hunger and thirst for righteousness, for they shall be filled" (Matt. 5:6). In the final analysis, there can be no personal contentment without spiritual contentment. There is a God-shaped void within all of us that only God can fill. He is both our hunger and satisfaction.

3. Vocational Contentment

Paul could testify, "To me, to live is Christ, and to die is gain" (Phil. 1:21). For him, life, even in a Roman prison, was fulfilling! His very captivity worked out to "the furtherance of the gospel" (Phil. 1:12). Christ is to be the Christian's entire life; he is to be absorbed and wrapped up in him. Every day with Jesus means contentment.

Illustration

Recently the residents of a Florida apartment building awoke to a terrifying sight outside their windows. The ground beneath the street in front of their building had literally collapsed, creating a massive depression that Floridians call a sinkhole. Tumbling into the ever-deepening pit were automobiles, pavement, sidewalks, and lawn furniture. The building itself would obviously be the next to go. Sinkholes occur, scientists say, when underground streams drain away during seasons of drought, causing the ground at the surface to lose its underlying support. Suddenly everything simply caves in, leaving people with a frightening suspicion that nothing—even the ground beneath their feet—is trustworthy. There are many people whose lives are like Florida's sinkholes. But for the Christian, there is contentment within, even when there is chaos everywhere else.[1]

II. A Life of Companionship

"I will never leave you nor forsake you" (Heb. 13:5). That is a tremendous word, and the more you study it—especially the meaning in the Greek—the more it thrills the heart. The companionship of the Lord Jesus is here distinguished as:

A. *A Personal Companionship*

The actual rendering here is: "He Himself has said, 'I will never leave you nor forsake you'" (Heb. 13:5). It would be wonderful to know that throughout the next twelve months the angel of the Lord would encamp around me (and I know that is true). It would be wonderful if God would send the archangel Gabriel to attend my path and clear the road ahead of me, keeping me safe from harm and danger. But God does not send an angel nor an archangel. He has said, "*I* will never leave you nor forsake you" (Heb. 13:5). We are assured here of the personal presence of the Lord Jesus every step of the way.

In Old Testament times, God came to people like Moses, Joshua, and David. And when the Lord Jesus was on earth he walked with men and women. But now, by his Spirit, he not only walks with us, he indwells us. Paul's testimony was, "I have been crucified with Christ; it is no longer I who live, but Christ lives in me" (Gal. 2:20). In Old Testament times, the Holy Spirit came upon various individuals. When he was grieved he departed from them. David had to cry, "Do not take your Holy Spirit from me" (Ps. 51:11), but now he abides with us forever (see John 14:16).

B. A Perpetual Companionship

"I will never leave you nor forsake you" (Heb. 13:5). However dark the night, we can be assured of his perpetual presence. In the original, there are no less than five negatives to express one positive truth: *"Never, never, in no wise* will I leave thee; *no, never* will I forsake thee!"

Illustration

Stephen Olford recounts how his father became lost on a hunting expedition in Africa. As he and a fellow colleague searched for game, night fell upon them and they were separated. The terrain was rough, dark, and dangerous. In the distance he could hear the call of the hyena, and near him the hiss of a snake. A sense of loneliness swept over him, as he faced the possibility of death. Then lifting his heart to the Lord in prayer, he said, "Hast thou not said, 'I will never leave thee, nor forsake thee'? I count upon that promise." Then came words he later penned in his Bible:

> Although I may feel lonely,
> Alone I cannot be;
> For He who loves me dearly;
> Will never forsake me.

How wonderful to be assured of the perpetual companionship of the Lord Jesus!

III. A Life of Courage

"The LORD is my helper; I will not fear. What can man do to me?" (Heb. 13:6). Contentment, companionship, and courage: these are the three essentials for every day of every month of every year. These words of verse 6, or similar words, occur four times in the Old Testament and can be summed up this way. Here is courage to face:

A. The Eventualities of Life

"We may boldly say: 'The LORD is my helper; I will not fear'" (Heb. 13:6). As men and women face a new year there is often a fearfulness of the *unknown*. People say, "What worries me is the fear of the unknown. What of tomorrow?" But if you know the presence of the Lord Jesus in your life you will have courage to face the eventualities of life, the unknown.

Here are two examples. The first is the story of Jacob. You will remember how, having deceived his brother, he ran for his life, and when night overtook him he lay down, with a stone for his pillow, and went fast asleep. Then God gave him a vision of a ladder stretching up to heaven, and the divine purposes for his life were unfolded to him. God said to him, "I am with you and will keep you wherever you go" (Gen. 28:15). As he went into the unknown, Jacob was assured of the presence of God, who promised to be with him and give him courage.

The second example is that of Moses giving his final message to the children of Israel. Having set before them life and death, he told them that whatever the opposition they would face in Canaan they could be assured of the presence and blessing of God, if they kept his commandments. His words were, "Be strong and of good courage, do not fear nor be afraid of them; for the LORD your God, He is the One who goes with you. He will not leave you nor forsake you" (Deut. 31:6). And if we are in the will of God we need not fear the eventualities of life.

Illustration

Gerhard Frost tells this story in his book, *The Color of Night:* "As a very young child, my greatest fear was of darkness. At times it even kept me awake. My father's study was just across the hall where often he would be at work at my bedtime. In a moment of panic I would cry out, frantic for a response. And the response always came: 'Go to sleep, I'm right here!' With this assurance I would rest. My father didn't bring a light—I would have liked that—but he gave me something better, the assurance of his loving presence. A light would have left me alone. In real need, it couldn't satisfy. Presence, loving presence, is what I craved."[2]

B. The Responsibilities of Life

"We may boldly say: 'The LORD is my helper; I will not fear'" (Heb. 13:6). People fear not only the eventualities of life, the unknown, but the responsibilities of life, the *known.* They know what devolves upon them, and they tremble and fear. Thank God, however, with the presence of the Lord Jesus we can face our responsibilities with courage.

Again we have two illustrations. The first is when God broke through to Joshua, a young man who followed the Lord wholly, and said to him, "Moses My servant is dead. Now therefore, arise. . . . Be strong and of good courage; do not be afraid, nor be dismayed, for the LORD your God is with you wherever you go" (Josh. 1:2, 9). As he considered the many responsibilities before him—the leadership, the administration, the incompatibility of personalities, the grumbling host—

he might well have felt like withdrawing from such a task; but being assured of God's presence he went forward with courage.

Then there was David, a man after God's own heart. Because he was a man of battle and of blood he was not allowed to build the temple. So he handed over the responsibility to Solomon his son, instructing him to finish all the work for the service of the house of the Lord. To hearten Solomon, David said, "Be strong and of good courage, and do it; do not fear nor be dismayed, for the LORD God—my God—will be with you. He will not leave you nor forsake you" (1 Chron. 28:20).

Therefore, to meet the eventualities and responsibilities of life we need the courage that comes through the knowledge of the presence of the Lord Jesus.

Conclusion

Someone may be asking, "How can I know the presence of the Lord Jesus in my life?" Go back to Exodus 33 and read those matchless words of God to Moses: "My Presence will go with you, and I will give you rest." Then back comes Moses to God, saying, "If Your Presence does not go with us, do not bring us up from here" (14-15). How can you know his presence? In dramatic symbolism, God says to Moses, "If you want to know my continual presence to lead this great host, stand upon a rock. I will hide you in the cleft of the rock, and I will pass by you and show you how you may know my presence every day of your life."

In terms of the New Testament, we know that the rock speaks of Christ, and standing upon the rock is personal faith in Christ. He was risen for us at Calvary. As we look into his face each of us can say:

> Rock of Ages, cleft for me,
> Let me hide myself in Thee . . .
>
> Augustus M. Toplady

Will you hide in the Rock now? If you do, the Lord Jesus will become to you a living, bright reality. You will be able to say:

> He lives, he lives,
> Christ Jesus lives today!
> He walks with me and talks with me
> along life's narrow way . . .[3]

and you will know what it is to have a life of contentment, companionship, and courage through his abiding presence.

4

Palm Sunday: *Behold Your King*
Matthew 21:1–11

"Rejoice greatly, O daughter of Zion; shout, O daughter of Jerusalem; behold, thy King cometh unto thee: he is just, and having salvation; lowly, and riding upon an ass" (Zech. 9:9 KJV).

Introduction

Without question, the message of Palm Sunday is the message of the King. When the Lord Jesus rode into Jerusalem on that first Palm Sunday he offered himself as King to the nation of Israel. But as you know, he was rejected—so much so that he sat upon that mountain, and with a loud voice cried, "O Jerusalem, Jerusalem, . . . how often would I have gathered thy children together, even as a hen gathereth her chickens under her wings, and ye would not! Behold, your house is left unto you desolate" (Matt. 23:37–38 KJV). In A.D. 70 that city was razed to the ground, thus fulfilling the prophecy of our Lord.

But more than that, he came to the temple, and he found not only those who were rejecting him, but those who were robbing him, their King. Remember how he cleansed the temple and said, "My house shall be called the house of prayer; but ye have made it a den of thieves" (Matt. 21:13 KJV)? God has called each of us to be his temple, and he will never be satisfied until he is crowned as undisputed and unrivaled King in our lives.

In considering our text in Zechariah 9:9, we recognize three aspects of our Lord's sovereign rule:

I. The Majesty of the King

"Rejoice greatly, O daughter of Zion; shout, O daughter of Jerusalem; behold, thy King cometh unto thee: he is just, and . . . lowly" (9:9 KJV). Those two tremendous words "just" and "lowly" comprehend the vision of the King that we are to behold.

A. The Majesty of His Righteousness

"He is just" (9:9), or more accurately, "He is righteous." Repressive governments and heads of state today are rightly being challenged concerning human rights. Man longs for a righteousness and justice which will be enacted or enforced only when Jesus Christ reigns on the throne of the universe. One day he will hold the scepter of universal empire and he will reign as King of Kings and Lord of Lords.

Amplify
Expound and enlarge on Isaiah 9:6–7.

B. The Majesty of His Lowliness

"Behold, thy King . . . he is lowly" (9:9 KJV). The genius of greatness is the ability to condescend. Man may aspire, but only God condescends. The greatest moment in history, so far as condescension is concerned, was when God contracted to the measure of a woman's womb; when the eternal one was born in time. Men looked into the face of God, the lowly one, wrapped in swaddling clothes in the manger. Yet wonder of wonders, he was born a King. Men are never *born* as kings, but as princes. But Jesus was born a King. He was the lowly one, but today we see him in his holy majesty. No potentate, no monarch, no head of state, has ever lived to lift our eyes to such holiness or bring our eyes down to such lowliness. Only Jesus Christ was fully God and fully man.

Amplify
Show that greatness comes by way of humility (see Phil. 2:5–11).

II. The Mastery of the King

"Behold, thy King . . . riding upon an ass, and upon a colt the foal of an ass" (9:9 KJV). We have seen that the King riding upon an ass was a symbol of lowliness. But it was also a symbol of peaceful entry into that great city of Jerusalem. From Matthew's narrative we learn something of the mastery of this King. He was the master of all the universe—the master of creation, the master of the winds and waves, the master of the animal creation, and what he did on that occasion illustrates the mastery he desires to exercise in your life and mine.

A. As King He Commandeered the Colt

He told his disciples, "Go into the village over against you, and straightway ye shall find an ass tied, and a colt with her: loose them, and bring them unto me. And if any man say ought unto you, ye shall say, The Lord hath need of them" (Matt. 21:2–3). He claimed his mount decisively and no one asked any questions; they immediately released the donkey for his use. This is a beautiful picture of the claim that God has upon your life. It is a threefold claim because he made you (Ps. 100:3), he bought you (1 Cor. 6:19–20), and he wants you (Matt. 21:3; Mark 11:3).

Illustration

Traveling from his own province through Germany on his way to the city of Paris, Count Zinzendorf, then a young man, halted at the town of Dusseldorf where there was a fine collection of paintings. He entered the art gallery to spend an hour or two admiring the works of some of the great masters. Coming to a picture of Christ suffering on the cross, he stood transfixed before the scene and read the words that the artist, Steinberg, had added to his painting: "All this I did for thee. What hast thou done for Me?" This was the turning point of his life. Abandoning his journey to Paris, he returned to his home and consecrated himself to the claims of the Lord Jesus Christ. Devoting himself and his wealth to the master's service, he became the leader of the Moravian brethren (1 Cor. 6:20; Gal. 2:20).

B. As King He Controlled the Colt

"Behold, thy King cometh . . . riding upon an ass" (Zech. 9:9 KJV). That in itself was a miracle. It takes eight weeks to break in a colt, and possibly another eight weeks or longer to train the young animal to behave in a crowd. With palms waving, with children singing, with men and women shouting, with the noisy confusion that must have occurred on that road into Jerusalem, Jesus rode majestically upon that colt into the city. He was the creature's master; he controlled it completely.

Illustration

Tom Rees tells of a jockey who attended a Palm Sunday service in an Anglican church in England. He was disgusted with himself over the sins in his life that he couldn't control. As the story of the triumphal entry into Jerusalem was read, his attention was arrested. He sat there utterly amazed as he thought about how that donkey was commandeered and mounted, unbroken and untrained as he was, by the Lord Jesus who rode him calmly through all the noise and confusion of the city. He recalled the hours he had spent in training colts and horses, and then he thought of himself. If Jesus Christ could quietly and quickly control a colt, surely he could master his life. And there, in the back of that Anglican church, the jockey was soundly converted.

Only Jesus Christ is able to bring every thought into the captivity of obedience to Christ (2 Cor. 10:5). Only he can bring the explosive energies of youth under his control and channel them to his higher purposes. Only he can control the mind, heart, will, and body. Behold the majesty of your King; submit to the mastery of your King!

III. The Ministry of the King

"Rejoice greatly, O daughter of Zion; shout, O daughter of Jerusalem; behold, thy King cometh unto thee . . . having salvation" (9:9 KJV), (or more literally, "bringing salvation"). The purpose for which Jesus came into the world was to bring salvation to men and women. Paul refers to this when he writes to Titus: "The grace of God that bringeth salvation hath appeared to all men" (Titus 2:11 KJV). And remember, when the Lord Jesus was born he was called Jesus, "for he shall save his people from their sins" (Matt. 1:21). The Lord Jesus stands outside the door of your heart, waiting to bring salvation to you. And as we look upon this world of ours, with all its tumult, division, and injustice, we realize that what it needs is not so much education or reformation or litigation, but salvation.

A. He Brings Salvation from the Penalty of Sin

"This is a faithful saying, and worthy of all acceptation, that Christ Jesus came into the world to save sinners" (1 Tim. 1:15 KJV).

Amplify
Show that salvation, first of all, is from the penalty of sin (see Rom. 3:23; 6:23; 10:13).

B. He Brings Salvation from the Power of Sin

"For the preaching of the cross is to them that perish foolishness; but unto us which are [being] saved, it is the power of God" (1 Cor. 1:18 KJV). It takes power to conquer power.

Exegete
Use 1 Corinthians 1:18 to describe the continuous process of salvation in the believer's life as we are being delivered from Satan's constant attacks by God's overcoming power.

C. He Brings Salvation from the Presence of Sin

"So Christ was once offered to bear the sins of many; and unto them that look for him shall he appear the second time without sin unto salvation" (Heb. 9:28 KJV). Then we shall be "like him"—"without sin."

Amplify
Show what Christ's appearance for the "second time" will mean for the believer. Use such verses as Romans 13:11–14; 1 Thessalonians 4:16–17, etc.

Conclusion

We have looked at the majesty of the King—his righteousness and lowliness. We have looked at the mastery of the King as he commandeered and controlled that young colt. We have looked at the ministry of the King, bringing a salvation that deals with the past, the present, and the future. What a King! Will you swing wide the door of your life and welcome him in as King of Kings and Lord of Lords?

5

Easter Sunday: *The Gospel of the Resurrection*
1 Corinthians 15:1–20

"Christ died . . . was buried, and . . . rose again the third day according to the scriptures" (15:3–4 KJV).

Introduction

In John Masefield's drama *The Trial of Jesus,* there is a striking passage in which the Roman centurion in command of the soldiers at the cross comes back to Pilate to hand in his report of the day's work. After the report is given, Pilate's wife beckons to the centurion and begs him to tell how the prisoner died. When the story has been told, she suddenly asks, "Do you think he is dead?" "No, lady," answers the centurion, "I don't." "Then where is he?" To which the Roman replies, "Let loose in the world, lady, where . . . no one can stop his truth."

And so it proved, for as soon as Jesus was risen and ascended, he empowered his disciples to make known the gospel of the resurrection throughout the whole of the then-known world.

The gospel of the resurrection is an indisputable fact, an indispensable faith, and an irresistible force. Perhaps nobody sets this out as clearly as does the great apostle Paul in that classic fifteenth chapter of 1 Corinthians. To him, the resurrection of the Lord Jesus was:

I. An Indisputable Fact

"Moreover, brethren, I declare unto you the gospel . . . how that Christ died for our sins according to the scriptures; and that he was buried, and that he rose again the third day according to the scriptures" (15:1, 3–4 KJV). With the perception of a theologian and the brilliance of a logician, Paul declares that the resurrection of our Lord Jesus Christ was, first of all:

A. A Fact of Prophecy

Christ "rose again the third day according to the scriptures" (15:4). What an arresting phrase this is— "according to the scriptures"! What did Paul mean? Quite obviously, since there was no New Testament in those days, he was referring to what we call our Old Testament. Paul was a student of those Hebrew Scriptures, and from his familiarity with them he could declare with categorical impressiveness that Christ "rose again the third day according to the scriptures" (15:4 KJV). In other words, the law, the psalms, and the prophets all predicted the resurrection of our Lord Jesus Christ; see the law (Gen. 3:15), the psalms (Ps. 16:10–11; also Acts 2:25–31), and the prophets (Isa. 53:10–11). Against the background of such Old Testament predictions Paul announces, "I declare unto you the gospel which I preached unto you . . . how that Christ died for our sins according to the scriptures; . . . and that he rose again the third day according to the scriptures" (15:1, 3–4 KJV). The resurrection of the Savior is a fact of prophecy.

B. A Fact of History

"Christ died for our sins . . . and . . . rose again" (15:3–4 KJV). Dr. F. F. Bruce points out that these words of the apostle Paul constitute one of the earliest pieces of documentary evidence concerning the resurrection of our Lord Jesus Christ. This statement of fact is dated less than twenty-five years after the Easter event. So impressive was this supporting evidence that it affected every one who heard it. Among the tens of thousands who were transformed by the gospel of the resurrection, Paul names three such witnesses in this very chapter—Peter (v. 5), James (v. 7), and Paul himself, (v. 8).

> **Illustration**
> Sir Edward Clarke (1841–1931), English lawyer and politician, has attested: "As a lawyer I have made a prolonged study of the evidence for the events of the resurrection. To me the evidence is conclusive, and over and over again in the High Court I have secured the verdict on evidence not nearly so compelling."[1]

II. An Indispensable Faith

Proclaims the apostle: "If Christ be not risen, then is our preaching vain, and your faith is also vain. . . . And if Christ be not raised, your faith is vain; ye are yet in your sins. . . . If in this life only we have hope in Christ, we are of all men most miserable" (15:14, 17, 19 KJV). In these words we have the apostle's estimate of the significance and value of the pivotal event we commemorate on Easter Sunday. Everything depends upon this central fact—a risen Christ. If Christ was not raised, then our preaching is empty, our faith is false, and we are in a state of abject misery.

A. Faith in the Preaching of the Christ

"If Christ be not risen, then is our preaching vain, and your faith is also vain" (15:14 KJV). In the last analysis, preaching represents the word of Christ. Everything that Jesus ever said during his earthly ministry must be judged in the light of the resurrection, for if he did not rise from the dead, how can we trust the words he spoke? How can we believe the claims he made? How can we aspire to the standards he set? In other words, if Christ was not raised, then both our preaching and our faith are vain. But Christ *is* risen, and as a result, every single word Jesus spoke rings with authority and vibrates with life; we can trust him implicitly.

> **Illustration**
> Alfred Lord Tennyson met General William Booth while both were out walking. "General," said Tennyson, "what is the news this morning?" "The news, sir," replied Booth, "is that Christ died for our sins and rose for our justification!" "Ah," replied the poet, "that is old news, and new news, and good news."[2]

B. Faith in the Power of the Cross

"And if Christ be not raised, your faith is vain; ye are yet in your sins" (15:17 KJV). If Jesus Christ never rose from the dead, then Calvary means nothing at all; other men have been crucified, and Jesus must be numbered among them. On the other hand, if he truly rose from the dead, then Calvary represents the unique redemptive act of God, providing forgiveness and salvation for men and women like you and me. Because he rose we can say that Christ "was delivered for our offenses, and was raised again for our justification" (Rom. 4:25 KJV). There is forgiveness and pardon through the blood of the cross because the resurrection of Jesus Christ invests that death with a saving significance. Peter knew this from personal experience. That is why he could write that we are "begotten . . . again unto a lively hope by the resurrection of Jesus Christ from the dead" (1 Peter 1:3 KJV).

Illustration

Henry Louis Mencken (1880–1956), American author and critic, was an irreverent and vicious cynic to the end. He once declared, "Either Jesus arose from the dead or he did not. If he did, then Christianity becomes plausible; if he did not, then it is sheer nonsense." No, not sheer nonsense, but rather *false* and *powerless*. False, because Jesus said he would rise. If he did not rise, then he and all the apostles are found liars. Powerless, because he is not alive to make good his promises. If Christ was not raised, we Christians are yet in our sins. But thank God, that is not so. Christ is risen indeed, is alive forevermore, and holds the keys of hell and of death.

C. Faith in the Prospect of the Church

"If in this life only we have hope in Christ, we are of all men most miserable" (15:19 KJV). When Jesus Christ was here upon earth, he said to his disciples, "I will build my church; and the gates of hell shall not prevail against it" (Matt. 16:18 KJV). This prediction was fulfilled on the day of Pentecost, when the nucleus of that Christian church was brought into being. Indeed, it is a fact of history that belief in the resurrection brought the church to birth. And when the church dispersed from Jerusalem to conquer the earth, it was the resurrection message that was the driving power behind it. If Christ had not physically and factually risen, the church which bears his name would have perished long ago, for numbers of fierce attacks—social, political, and intellectual—have been launched against her down through the centuries. Often, indeed, she has seemed doomed and dead, and the grave diggers, like Hume, Voltaire, and others, have been busy; but always, like her Savior, she has risen from the grave and rolled away the stone. Only the fact of the resurrection of Jesus can explain the existence of the church of the living God.

What is more, the church has a glorious destiny, for beyond this life she has an eternal future. Christ, who gave himself for the church, is coming back again to rapture his church, to present her without spot, or blemish, or defect, before the glory of the Father (Eph. 5:27).

Illustration
An anonymous writer has said that "the church of Christ owes its very existence to the fact that in this . . . graveyard of the world there is one gaping tomb, one rent sepulchre."

III. An Irresistible Force

"Thanks be to God, which giveth us the victory through our Lord Jesus Christ" (15:57 KJV). If the opening of this amazing chapter deals with the fact of the resurrection, and the heart of the chapter presents the faith of the resurrection, then the concluding verses speak of the force of the resurrection (see 15:54–57).

A. A Revealed Force

Paul states this succinctly when he says that Jesus Christ was "declared to be the Son of God with power, according to the spirit of holiness, by the resurrection from the dead" (Rom. 1:4 KJV). Christ made some extraordinary claims before he went to the cross. Likening his body to the earthly temple, he announced, "Destroy this temple, and in three days I will raise it up" (John 2:19 KJV; see also John 10:17–18). Such statements as these were vindicated when the stone was rolled away and the grave was revealed to be empty. In the triumph of the resurrection the Son of God exemplified every other manifestation of divine power, including the creation of the world.

Illustration

A father and mother lost three children in one week by diphtheria. Only the little three-year-old girl escaped. On Easter morning, the father, mother, and child were in Sunday school. The father was the superintendent. He led the school in worship and read the Easter message from the Bible without a break in his voice. Many in the school were weeping, but the faces of the father and mother remained serene and calm. "How can they do it?" men and women asked each other as they left the church. A fifteen-year-old boy, walking home with his father said, "Father, I guess the superintendent and his wife really believe all of it—Easter you know!" "Of course," answered the father, "all Christians believe it!" "Not as they believe," said the boy.

Do you really believe in Easter? Is the resurrected Christ your hope? Can you say with the apostle Paul, "Death is swallowed up in victory. O death, where is thy sting? O grave, where is thy victory? . . . Thanks be to God, which giveth us the victory through our Lord Jesus Christ" (1 Cor. 15:54–57 KJV)?[3]

B. A Released Force

He said to his disciples, "But ye shall receive power, after that the Holy Ghost is come upon you: and ye shall be witnesses unto me both in Jerusalem, and in all Judea, and in Samaria, and unto the uttermost part of the earth" (Acts 1:8 KJV). It is well to remember that the teaching of Jesus was complete before he ever went to the cross. But the disciples were unable to preach his truth. They had the theory but they lacked the power. But on the basis of the cross, the resurrection, and the ascension, Jesus poured out his Spirit, in liberated resurrection life, and those weak disciples, filled with his life, boldly went everywhere making the Savior known. They could now preach with fearlessness and suffer even unto death.

Conclusion

Face up to this gospel of the resurrection as a fact, a faith, and a force in Christ—to believe and receive. And having believed and received, go out to a lost world and tell men and women that Jesus died and rose again to be the Savior of sinners.

Labor Day Sunday: *Spiritual Stewardship*
1 Peter 4:7–11

"As each one has received a gift, minister it to one another, as good stewards of the manifold grace of God" (4:10).

Introduction

It is important to notice the urgency with which Peter challenges his readers concerning spiritual stewardship. "The end of all things is at hand," he says (4:7). Christ is coming, the days of earthly opportunity are numbered; therefore he encourages them to use the gifts God has given them with soberness, watchfulness, prayerfulness, and love.

The office of a steward, in Peter's day, was to administer and dispense his master's goods for the due maintenance of the household. As applied to us, the household is the church of God, and we are responsible to him as good stewards. How are we fulfilling this high and holy task? If the Lord were to call us home today would we be able to give a good accounting of our stewardship? It's something to think about and to adjust our lifestyle accordingly.

In the verses before us we have:

I. The Steward's Spiritual Endowment

"As each one has received a gift, minister it to one another, as good stewards of the manifold grace of God" (4:10). It is clear from this statement that endowments for stewards are apportioned by God and accountable to God.

A. They Are Apportioned by God

"As each one has received a *gift* . . ." (4:10). This term "gift" is represented by nine different words in the Greek which have three shades of meaning: "a present," "an offering to God," and "a personal endowment." The last is undoubtedly the "gift" of our text. This endowment is the gift of the Holy Spirit, whom God gives to us at the new birth. He not only constitutes the believer a steward, but he also sanctifies all natural and spiritual gifts for the purpose of stewardship alone. All endowments are freely, impartially, and unconditionally assigned through the manifold grace of God. Our God has no favorites. The gifts he distributes are varied, just as every individual is different one from the other. Let us earnestly seek to discover our gift(s) by praying Paul's prayer, "Lord, what do You want me to do?" (Acts 9:6).

Amplify

While everyone has some spiritual gift(s) (see 1 Cor. 12; Eph. 4:8–12) no one has all these gifts. Yet there are certain other "gifts" that each of us can give throughout the year:

The gift of praise—Appropriate mention, right in front of the other fellow, of superior qualities, or of a job or deeds well done.

The gift of consideration—Putting yourself in the other's shoes and thus providing your genuine understanding of his side of the case.

The gift of concession—Humbly saying at just the right point, "I am sorry, you are right and I am wrong."

The gift of gratitude—Never forgetting to say "thank you" and never failing to mean it.

The gift of attention—When the other fellow speaks, listen attentively. If his words are directed to you personally, meet his eye squarely.

The gift of inspiration—Plant seeds of courage and action in the other person's heart.

The gift of your personal presence—In sickness, in trouble, or in great joy, there is nothing quite equal to your personal expression of sympathy or congratulations.

Resolve to give these gifts each day. You will be pleasantly surprised at what you will receive in return.[1]

B. They Are Accountable to God

"Minister . . . to one another, as good stewards of the manifold grace of God" (4:10). No one receives the endowment as his own: he is but a steward. When he offers his gift to the church, it is not as a benefactor, but as a servant dispensing his master's goods in the interests of the community. We cannot assume these endowments for ourselves, or bury them in the ground (see Matt. 25:18, 25–26). They are the Lord's goods, and therefore they must be employed as he directs. "It is required in stewards that one be found faithful [since] . . . each of us shall give account of himself to God" (1 Cor. 4:2; Rom. 14:12).

According to the New Testament, a steward's accountability will be tested by three questions:

1. *Were you faithful* with your endowments?—"Who then is that faithful and wise steward . . . that ser-

vant whom his master will find so doing when he comes"? (Luke 12:42–43).
2. *Were you efficient* with your endowments?—"Minister . . . to one another, as good stewards" (1 Peter 4:10).
3. *Were you blameless* with your endowments?—"For a bishop must be blameless, as a steward of God" (Titus 1:7).

The steward's endowments are accountable to God. Let us see to it that we are found faithful, efficient, and blameless.

Illustration

A young man applied for a job as a farmhand. When asked for his qualifications, he said, "I can sleep when the wind blows." This puzzled the farmer, but he took a liking to the young man and hired him. A few days later, the farmer and his wife were awakened in the night by a violent storm. They quickly began to check things out to see if all was secure. They found that the shutters of the farmhouse had been securely fastened. A good supply of logs had been set next to the fireplace. The farm implements had been placed in the storage shed, safe from the elements. The tractor had been moved into the garage. The barn had been properly locked. All was well. Even the animals were calm. It was then that the farmer grasped the meaning of the young man's words, "I can sleep when the wind blows." Because the farmhand had performed his work loyally and faithfully when the skies were clear, he was prepared for the storm when it broke. Consequently, when the wind blew, he had no fear. He was able to sleep in peace.[2]

II. The Steward's Spiritual Employment

"Let him *speak* as the oracles of God . . . let him *do* it as with the ability which God supplies" (4:11). It is quite clear from these words that the Christian steward has a twofold employment, namely:

A. To Speak the Word of God

"If [or when] anyone speaks, let him speak as the oracles of God" (4:11). This exhortation implies a complete surrender of the speaker's self to the Holy Spirit so that both in public and in private his messages carry the authority of "thus saith the Lord." This was true of *Christ*. "He taught . . . as one having authority, and not as the scribes" (Mark 1:22). *Paul's* speech and preaching were "in demonstration of the Spirit and of power" (1 Cor. 2:4). *Peter* declared: "We cannot but speak the things which we have seen and heard" (Acts 4:20).

The steward's employment covers the three forms of vocal expression: (1) *the ministry of prayerful preaching:* the *evangelist* (see Eph. 4:11); (2) *the ministry of prayerful exhorting:* speaking to edification and comfort, for example, the *pastor* (see Eph. 4:11); (3) *the ministry of prayerful teaching:* declaring the whole counsel of God, for example, the *teacher* (see Eph. 4:11). As one possessed of a power and a message not his own, the Christian steward who is called to speak as the oracles of God must not, cannot, will not, keep silent. His burden will be that of the apostle who declared, "For if I preach the gospel, I have nothing to boast of, for necessity is laid upon me; yes, woe is me if I do not preach the gospel!" (1 Cor. 9:16).

> **Illustration**
>
> When David Hume, the infidel, was charged with inconsistency in going to listen to John Brown, the godly Scottish minister of Haddington, he replied: "I don't believe all that he says, but he does, and once a week I like to hear a man who believes what he says. Why, whatever I think, the man preaches as though he thought the Lord Jesus Christ was at his elbow."[3]

B. To Support the Work of God

"If anyone ministers, let him do it as with the ability which God supplies" (4:11). This does not mean ministering in the sense of speaking the Word of God. It rather denotes the supporting of the work of God. All such ministry, to be real, must be bathed in prayer. The apostle says, "In everything by prayer and supplication, with thanksgiving, let your requests be made known to God" (Phil. 4:6). The threefold expression of this service includes:

1. THE SUPPORT OF CONSECRATED NATURAL ABILITY

"As each one has received a gift, [so] minister it to one another" (4:10). By natural ability, I mean those manifold gifts with which God has endowed us, such as: writing, typing, organizing, leading, catering, nursing, and so on. Have we dedicated our natural abilities to God? If not, we must heed Paul's call to full surrender: "I beseech you therefore, brethren, by the mercies of God, that you present your bodies a living sacrifice, holy, acceptable to God, which is your reasonable service" (Rom. 12:1).

2. THE SUPPORT OF CONSECRATED MATERIAL ABILITY

It is recorded of certain women who loved the Lord Jesus that they "provided for him from their substance" (Luke 8:3). Here is a wonderful scope for hospitality in its widest sense. Have we ever noticed the emphasis that the New Testament places on the ministry of hospitality—"to one another without grumbling" (1 Peter 4:9). What an opportunity this is for young and old! Is the home consecrated to God? Is it a center of prayer, fellowship, and witness (see Rom. 12:13; 1 Tim. 3:2; Titus 1:8)?

3. THE SUPPORT OF CONSECRATED FINANCIAL ABILITY

"If anyone ministers, let him do it as with the ability which God *supplies*" (4:11). The verb "supplies" or "gives," in its original classical meaning, carries the thought of paying the expenses to put on a stage play, which at Athens was a public burden. Wealthier citizens took turns in underwriting this expense.

This seems to suggest that it is the wealthy Christian who should bear the main financial burden for evangelistic crusades, church activities, and the relief of the poor. Such a well-to-do person should not be regarded as the patron of the church, but rather a responsible steward fulfilling his rightful employment.

Is our money consecrated to God? Remember, our promises to God should be as binding as those we make to a bank. If there were less deceitful giving in the church today we would not be so busy burying the Ananiases and Sapphiras (see Acts 5:1–11)!

Amplify

If you give to charity while you are poor, you will eventually give in days of wealth. If you do not give while you are rich, you will eventually abstain from giving because of poverty. God has willed that there be two hands in the matter of charity—one that gives and one that receives. Thank God that yours is the hand that gives. Say not, "I will miss what I give." Be like the sheep who give their wool and have no less the next year because they have given.[4]

III. The Steward's Spiritual Endeavor

"That in all things God may be glorified through Jesus Christ, to whom belong the glory and the dominion forever and ever. Amen" (4:11). Here we have the true endeavor of all spiritual stewardship: "That . . . God may be glorified through Jesus Christ" (4:11). This means that:

A. Christ Is Given His Rightful Place

"That in all things God may be glorified" (4:11). God is only glorified when Christ is made Lord—"Therefore

God also has highly exalted Him and given Him the name which is above every name, that at the name of Jesus every knee should bow, of those in heaven, and of those on earth, and of those under the earth, and that every tongue should confess that Jesus Christ is Lord, to the glory of God the Father" (Phil. 2:9–11).

> Lord of every thought and action,
> Lord to send and Lord to stay;
> Lord in speaking, writing, giving,
> Lord in all things to obey;
> Lord of all there is of me,
> Now and evermore to be.
>
> E. H. Swinstead[5]

The only stewardship which counts is that which is under the control of Jesus Christ as Lord. Are there departments in our stewardship marked "private"? We must remember, he is either Lord of all, or not Lord at all!

B. Christ Is Given His Rightful Praise

"To whom belong the glory and the dominion forever and ever. Amen" (4:11). The supreme endeavor of the genuine steward is not only to give Christ his rightful place in everything, but to give him the praise that is due. The Lord Jesus only receives praise when we speak or support as stewards, out of hearts of unfeigned love, giving thanks in all things and under all circumstances—"Whoever offers praise glorifies Me" (Ps. 50:23); and again: "Praise from the upright is beautiful" (Ps. 33:1). In peace, prosperity, and plenty, we readily crown him Lord and praise his name; but what about the other times when life isn't as rosy?

> When in prison—to sing praises (see Acts 16:25)
> When in fires—to glorify the Lord (see Isa. 24:15)
> When in temptation—to count it a joy (see James 1:2)
> When in death—to glorify God (see John 21:19)

Illustration

John Wesley was 88 years old when he died. On the last day of his life, [though] extremely weak, he astonished those around him with these words:

> I'll praise my Maker while I've breath;
> And when my voice is lost in death,
> Praise shall employ my nobler powers:
> My days of praise shall ne'er be past,
> While life, and thought, and being last,
> Or immortality endures.[6]

But there is an even greater thought in this endeavor of the steward. Christ given his rightful praise, in the last analysis, means fulfilling all that stewardship entails, and then turning to the master and saying,

> Though I've done my level best,
> Lord, my heart can never rest,
> Till before Thy feet I pour
> Every treasure of love's store.
> Only thus can I express
> All the praise within my breast.
>   Stephen F. Olford

Peter wraps up this thought of spiritual stewardship with the word "Amen"—even so let it be. Can you say that as well? That is the acid test of our true endeavor as stewards.

Conclusion

We shall never be fulfilled as Christians until we understand as well as undertake what the New Testament means by spiritual stewardship. As we have learned in this study, it is an endowment, an employment, and an endeavor made possible by the grace of God for the glory of God; and "man's chief end is to glorify God, and to enjoy him forever."

Thanksgiving Sunday:
The Duty of Thankfulness
Psalm 92:1–15

"It is good to give thanks to the LORD, and to sing praises to Your name, O Most High; To declare Your lovingkindness in the morning, and Your faithfulness every night" (92:1–2).

Introduction

Psalm 92 is a hymn of gratitude. The author—whoever he may have been—goes beyond formal theology to express his profound thanksgiving to a God who had become intensely real to him. As we examine the first five verses, in particular, we learn that for the true child of God:

I. The Duty of Thankfulness Is a Moral Necessity

"It is good to give thanks to the LORD" (92:1). Such a statement carries a serious implication with it. If it is a good thing to give thanks to the Lord then, quite obviously, it is a bad thing to withhold such gratitude. Sad to say, this is one of the prevalent sins of our time.

When the apostle Paul lists the stages in man's descent, from the true knowledge of God to vile wickedness, he names thanklessness as the source of all other sins. He phrases it this way: "because, although they knew God, they did not glorify Him as God, nor were thankful, but became . . ." (Rom. 1:21). Then follows one of the darkest descriptions of man's corrupt nature and practice.

Sir Walter Scott maintained that "ingratitude comprehended every vice." Shakespeare wrote of ingratitude as "the marble-hearted fiend." So the duty of thankfulness is a moral necessity because it is a good thing. The psalmist leaves us in no doubt as to why we should give thanks to the Lord:

A. We Must Gratefully Appreciate God's Blessings Which Are Behind Us

"For You, LORD, have made me glad through Your work" (92:4). The psalmist is taking a backward look and recounting how God had gladdened his heart through past blessings. And who can fail to agree with the psalmist in this respect? Think, for a moment, of:

1. PAST SPIRITUAL BLESSINGS

"For You, LORD, have made me glad through Your work" (92:4). Who among us can withhold praise to God as we think of his work in our lives whereby God became our Father, the Lord Jesus became our Savior, the Holy Spirit became our Comforter, the Bible became our guide, the church became our fellowship, and heaven became our home? Truly, we have to exclaim with the apostle Paul, "Blessed be the God and Father of our Lord Jesus Christ, who has blessed us with every spiritual blessing in the heavenly places in Christ" (Eph. 1:3). We sometimes sing,

"Count your many blessings, name them one by one," but, surely, this is an impossible task! God has so lavished his good hand upon us that we just have to cry, "For You, LORD, have made me glad through your work" (92:4). Do you thank the Lord Jesus every day for saving your soul?

Illustration

Some years ago the late Dr. Donald G. Barnhouse was traveling from Alabama to Florida. Feeling a tire going flat, he pulled to the side of the road and inwardly groaned at the thought of removing the hundreds of books in the trunk, so as to reach his spare tire. Seeing a jeep coming over the hill, he hailed the driver and offered him money to fix the flat. The big, strapping fellow was soon hard at work. When he expressed curiosity about the books, Dr. Barnhouse told him he was a preacher. The man said, "My wife would be interested, but I'm not interested in those things." All the time the man worked his dog stood close to him, licking him every minute. Now and again the man stopped to pat it. The man shared how the dog had once saved his life by pulling him out of quicksand and for that reason he was devoted to the dog. "It eats at my table and, though my wife does not like it, he sleeps at the foot of my bed." Looking into the man's face, Dr. Barnhouse commented, "How strange! The dog has saved your life from quicksand and you are devoted to it. Yet Christ has done more than the dog and you are not interested in Christ. You are in a worse plight than quicksand, from which Christ came to save you. The dog did not die for you, but Christ did; yet you thank the dog, but are not thankful to Christ." How that story ought to make us thank the Savior every moment for saving us from eternal perdition.

2. PAST SOCIAL BLESSINGS

"For You, LORD, have made me glad through Your work" (92:4). The psalmist tells us that "God sets the solitary in families" (Ps. 68:6). This is exactly what has happened to us. Whether we think of the circle of our family, our friends, or the fellowship of saints, just consider for a moment the enjoyment and enrichment that have been brought into our lives through the men and women, boys and girls, who have crossed our path. What a miserable world it would be without mothers and fathers, brothers and sisters, and the fellowship of the Christian church! The hymnist expresses it well:

> For the joy of human love,
> Brother, sister, parent, child,
> Friends on earth, and friends above,
> For all gentle thoughts and mild,
> Lord of all, to Thee we raise
> This our hymn of grateful praise.
>
> Folliott S. Pierpoint

3. PAST TEMPORAL BLESSINGS

"For You, LORD, have made me glad through Your work" (92:4); and again: "Bless the LORD, O my soul, and forget not all His benefits" (Ps. 103:2). The psalmist undoubtedly includes temporal blessings in the comprehensiveness of that little word "work"; and so must we. God's favor upon our homes, prosperity in our businesses, and health-giving food to our bodies, are all part of the divine work of Providence.

The Puritan writer, William Law, considered a thankful spirit an essential quality of sainthood. He wrote: "Would you know who is the greatest saint in the world? It is not he who prays most or fasts most; it is not he who gives alms or who is most eminent for temperance, chastity, or justice, but it is he who is always thankful to God, who receives everything as an instance of God's goodness, and has a heart always ready to praise God for it."

If we study this psalm carefully we shall notice

that there is not only a backward look for which we are to be thankful, but there is also a forward look:

B. We Must Gratefully Anticipate God's Blessings Which Are Before Us

"I will triumph in the works of Your hands. O LORD, how great are Your works! Your thoughts are very deep" (92:4–5). This is a thrilling statement! The psalmist has looked back with gladness and gratitude because of the blessings God has lavished upon his life, but now with expectation he exults in the possibilities of the future. He says, "O LORD, how great are Your works! Your thoughts [more literally, designs and purposes] are very deep" (92:5). Whatever has been experienced in the past is not to be compared with what lies ahead.

Paul must have been thinking of words like this when he wrote, under the guidance of the Holy Spirit: "Eye has not seen, nor ear heard, Nor have entered into the heart of man the things which God has prepared for those who love Him" (1 Cor. 2:9). Thank God, there are no limitations attached to God's purpose of blessings, except those we impose by unbelief. It is one thing to drop on our knees and give thanks to God for blessings past and present, but it is quite another matter to thank God in faith for his great work and deep purposes that he has in store for us.

Major Ian Thomas once said at a conference, "A prayer which does not give thanks to God for what he is going to do is not a prayer of faith, for faith is more than asking: it is taking from the hand of God and saying 'thank you.'"

> How good is the God we adore,
> Our faithful, unchangeable Friend,
> Whose love is as great as His pow'r,
> And knows neither measure nor end.

'Tis Jesus, the First and the Last,
Whose Spirit shall guide us safe home;
We'll praise Him for all that is past,
And trust Him for all that's to come.

J. Hart[1]

II. The Duty of Thankfulness Is a Major Activity

"It is good to give thanks to the LORD, and to sing praises to Your name, O Most High; to declare Your lovingkindness in the morning, and Your faithfulness every night" (92:1–2). Thankfulness is a major activity inasmuch as it engages the total man—spirit, soul, and body. The psalmist speaks here of:

A. Spiritual Thankfulness

"It is good to give thanks to the LORD" (92:1). There is a level of praying and praising which cannot be expressed in words. It is an activity of worship within the realm of the spirit. Paul speaks of it in his First Epistle to the Corinthians when he talks about praying with the spirit and singing with the spirit (see 1 Cor. 14:14–15). How the Father in heaven seeks such worship from his redeemed people! Do we know anything about this activity within the realm of our spirits?

Amplify

Next time you're having your Quiet Time, why not pick up your hymnal and use the words of a grand old hymn to express to the Lord something of the "wonder, love, and praise" felt in your own heart. It will quicken your own spirit as you wait on God.

B. Personal Thankfulness

"It is good . . . to sing praises to Your name, O Most High" (92:1). This is praising—not so much with the spirit as with the understanding (see 1 Cor. 14:15). It involves the use of our mental and vocal powers. "Man's chief end is to glorify God and to enjoy him forever," and there can be no greater activity than to sing praises to the name of the Most High God.

Although this psalm was used for public worship on the Sabbath day, its message contains a far wider application. We not only praise God with our lips when we stand up to sing in church, our lips should sound his glories wherever we find ourselves: in the home, in business, or in the world at large.

But even more important than the testimony of our lips is the thanksgiving of our lives. We must be able to say and mean, "For . . . me, to live is Christ" (Phil. 1:21); and again: "We should live soberly, righteously, and godly in the present age" (Titus 2:12). If what we are does not exalt the "name of the Most High," then what we say or sing is virtually worthless.

Amplify

In praising God with our understanding, let's be specific and intelligent in rendering our thanks. The words of a Swedish hymn, "Thanks to God," written by August Ludvig Storm, a Salvation Army officer, can help us in this regard. It is worth noting that the author gives thanks for many of the negative aspects of life—tears, storms, and pain. He himself experienced a partial paralysis from the age of thirty-seven.

Thanks to God

Thanks, O God, for boundless mercy from Thy gracious throne above;
Thanks for ev'ry need provided from the fullness of Thy love!
Thanks for daily toil and labor and for rest when shadows fall;
Thanks for love of friend and neighbor and Thy goodness unto all!

Thanks for thorns as well as roses, thanks for weakness and for health;

Thanks for clouds as well as sunshine, thanks for poverty and wealth!
Thanks for pain as well as pleasure—all Thou sendest day by day;
And Thy Word, our dearest treasure, shedding light upon our way.

Thanks, O God, for home and fireside, where we share our daily bread;
Thanks for hours of sweet communion, when by Thee our souls are fed!
Thanks for grace in time of sorrow and for joy and peace in Thee;
Thanks for hope today, tomorrow, and for all eternity!

C. Musical Thankfulness

"To declare Your lovingkindness in the morning, and Your faithfulness every night, on an instrument of ten strings" (92:2–3). The "instrument of ten strings," or psaltery, was a kind of harp that was used in the worship of God, both in the temple and in smaller groups throughout Old Testament times. The instrument symbolizes the outgoing of the total human personality in a ministry of praise. Those who played the harp were usually professional musicians, and their time was mostly spent morning and night strumming their praise to God, or in leading the worship of God's house.

What was true of those harpists should be equally true of our lives. Every day we should show forth the lovingkindness of our God, and every night we should celebrate his faithfulness. Our total beings should be a symphony of thankfulness. Only then will men and women come to believe that Christ is real to us.

When David describes his great deliverance in Psalm 40 he says, "[God] has put a new song in my mouth—Praise to our God; many will see it and fear, and will trust in the LORD" (v. 3).

When we think about musical thankfulness we are

reminded of Paul and Silas in that prison in Philippi. If ever men had a right to bemoan their sad lot, it was these two warriors of the cross. Even though beaten and bleeding, and put into the innermost cell of the prison where their feet were fastened in stocks, Luke tells us that "at midnight Paul and Silas were praying [worshiping] and singing hymns to God, and the prisoners were listening to them" (Acts 16:23–25). The word "listening" is a rare verb. It means "to listen with pleasure as to a recitation or music." It was a new experience for the prisoners and a wonderful testimony of Christian trustfulness and thankfulness. The result of such triumphant thankfulness was that a great earthquake shook the prison, so that the prisoners were released, and the jailer was saved! Paul reminds us that when we are filled with the Holy Spirit we make "melody in [our hearts] . . . to the Lord, giving thanks" (Eph. 5:19–20).

Conclusion

We have seen what constitutes the duty of thankfulness. It is a moral necessity and it is a major activity. Let us see to it that we remember to give thanks to the Lord, to sing praises unto his name, and to show forth his lovingkindness in the morning and his faithfulness every night. Only then shall we fulfill God's purpose in creation and redemption.

Part 2

Special Occasions

Baptism Service:
The Blessing of Obedience
*Matthew 3:13–17;
Luke 3:21–22; John 1:29–34*

Introduction

The one word which sums up the Christian life in its entirety is the term *obedience* (see Matt. 3:15). It is a word which characterized the life of the Lord Jesus Christ. In a striking passage in Hebrews 5:8–9 we read these words concerning him: "Though He was a Son, yet He learned obedience by the things which He suffered. And having been perfected, he became the author of eternal salvation to all who obey him." In Philippians 2, there are similar words to describe the self-emptying and condescension of the Son of God: "Let this mind be in you which was also in Christ Jesus, who, being in the form of God, did not consider it robbery to be equal with God, but made Himself of no reputation, taking the form of a servant, and coming in the likeness of men. And being found in appearance as a man, He humbled Himself and became obedient to the point of death, even the death of the cross" (vv. 5–8). So the master set the standard; we can do no less than seek the enabling of the Holy Spirit to live out, in terms of daily experience, the practice of obedience. Observe:

I. The Demands of Obedience

"Jesus answered and said . . . 'Permit it to be so now, for thus it is fitting for us to fulfill all righteousness'" (Matt. 3:15). Although there is a sense in which the baptism of our Lord Jesus Christ is unique and incomparable, there are principles of obedience in this act of our Savior which we do well to examine and emulate. As he faced his baptism, there were three demands which the Lord Jesus had to fulfill in order to please his Father in this matter of obedience:

A. The Reality of a True Confession

"Then Jesus came from Galilee to John at the Jordan to be baptized by him" (Matt. 3:13). Up until now the master had lived in relative obscurity. For 30 years he had lived humbly and worked industriously in the little town of Nazareth. Now God's hour had struck; it was time for him to enter upon his momentous ministry.

Like the priests of old who commenced their service for God with the cleansing of water, so Jesus presented himself for baptism on the banks of the river Jordan. This was his public confession. He was marking himself out to be both the Lamb of God and the Son of God. John the Baptist had been forewarned by God that one would appear whose very bearing, speech, and presence would distinguish him as the Redeemer of the world. How carefully this rugged preacher must have examined the faces of those who came to hear him preach in order that he might recognize the true Messiah! And then the day came when the Holy Spirit witnessed to him that here, indeed, was the Lamb of God and the Son of God.

Before his baptism, John said of Jesus: "Behold! The

Lamb of God who takes away the sin of the world!" (John 1:29). What a beautiful description of Jesus as he walked. A lamb speaks of sacrifice and submission, and of Jesus it is recorded that he was "led as a lamb to the slaughter, and as a sheep before its shearers is silent, so He opened not His mouth" (Isa. 53:7). But a lamb also speaks of separation. This animal is distinguished in the Old Testament as having the cloven hoof, suggestive of the separated walk. Is it any wonder the writer to the Hebrews could say that he was "holy, harmless, undefiled, separate from sinners"? (Heb. 7:26).

Jesus had no sins of his own to confess so he was qualified to identify himself with the human race in the ordinance of baptism. By stepping down into the waters of Jordan, he was declaring that he would die, be buried and rise again, for the redemption of mankind.

When we take our stand in baptism, we likewise declare that we intend to follow Jesus in a life of death and burial to self and of resurrection union with our glorified Lord. This is what Paul means when he says, "Therefore we were buried with Him through baptism into death, that just as Christ was raised from the dead by the glory of the Father, even so we also should walk in newness of life" (Rom. 6:4).

As Jesus emerged from the waters of baptism, the Spirit witnessed to John the Baptist that this was indeed the Son of God: "And John bore witness, saying, 'I saw the Spirit descending from heaven like a dove, and he remained upon Him. I did not know Him, but He who sent me to baptize with water said to me, "Upon whom you see the Spirit descending, and remaining on Him, this is He who baptizes with the Holy Spirit." And I have seen and testified that this is the Son of God'" (John 1:32–34).

If our confession in baptism is genuine, then we should be able to show to a skeptical world that we have become partakers of the divine nature. Although we cannot be called *the* Son of God, we can be known as the sons of God—"But as many as received Him, to them He gave the right to become children of God, even to those who believe in His name" (John 1:12; see Rom. 8:14, 16).

This is the reality of a true confession. There should be clearly seen in us the characteristics of the Lamb of God and the Son of God.

B. The Resoluteness of a True Submission

"Jesus answered and said to him, 'Permit it to be so now, for thus it is fitting for us to fulfill all righteousness'" (Matt. 3:15). When Jesus requested to be baptized, John forbade him saying, "I have need to be baptized by You, and are You coming to me?" (Matt. 3:14). It was then that Jesus answered in the language of true submission, "Permit it to be so now, for thus it is fitting for us to fulfill all righteousness" (Matt. 3:15). Here was:

1. WILLING SUBMISSION

"Permit it to be so now" (Matt. 3:15). He wanted nothing to hinder his obedience. How characteristic this was of our Lord's willing obedience and submission! Even before he came to earth we hear him saying, prophetically, "Behold, I come; in the scroll of the Book it is written of me. I delight to do Your will, O my God, and Your law is within my heart" (Ps. 40:7–8). During his ministry he spoke similar words: "My food is to do the will of Him who sent Me, and to finish His work" (John 4:34). And then we are reminded of the tremendous words he uttered in the Garden of Gethsemane as he agonized in prayer: "If it is possible, let this cup pass from Me; nevertheless, not as I will, but as You will" (Matt. 26:39). What submission!

Illustration

Can we willingly submit to God's plan for our lives? Look at the life of Dr. Albert Schweitzer, considered by many to be one of the greatest philanthropists of all time.

He was trying to settle on his life's work. He had so many abilities—for music, for medicine, for teaching—and was a master in each of those fields. There were uncounted opportunities for him. . . . What was God's plan for him? One day he was cleaning off his desk. Among the papers there was a . . . magazine of the Paris Missionary Society. . . . He glanced through it and noticed an article entitled, "The Needs of the Congo Mission." He read the article, and when he finished Dr. Schweitzer said, "My search is over." He was willing to lose himself in God's plan.[1]

2. WORTHY SUBMISSION

"Permit it to be so now, for thus it is *fitting* for us to fulfill all righteousness" (Matt. 3:15). To him, submission to the will of God was the most fitting thing in all the world. So often people perform the will of God as if they were doing him a favor. How can anyone descend to such impertinence as to even suggest such a thought? Anything less than the will of God is sin, whereas, to bow in willing submission to God's demands is not only right and proper, but worthy of our blessed Lord.

3. WHOLEHEARTED SUBMISSION

"Permit it to be so now, for thus it is fitting for us to fulfill *all* righteousness" (Matt. 3:15). Mark that little word *all*. In the life of the Lord Jesus every *i* was dotted and every *t* was crossed, in terms of his submission and obedience. Anything less than fulfilling all righteousness was not obedience to him.

The prophet Samuel could say, "To obey is better than sacrifice, and to heed than the fat of rams" (1 Sam. 15:22). Sacrifice and the fat of rams are meaningless offerings if there is not wholehearted obedience in the life.

Illustration

An aviation cadet on a practice flight was suddenly stricken with blindness. Frantically, he contacted the control tower. . . . His commanding officer radioed back, "Don't be afraid, just do what I tell you!" After being advised to keep circling the field until all was clear for a landing, the sightless pilot was instructed to begin losing altitude. As the aircraft approached the runway, the officer's voice called out encouragingly, "You're coming in right on target!" The cadet, giving unquestioned obedience to his commander, brought the plane down safely.[2]

C. The Responsiveness of a True Devotion

"This is My beloved Son, in whom I am well pleased" (Matt. 3:17). God could have never expressed these words concerning his beloved Son unless there was the responsiveness of true devotion in his heart. If we examine this glorious commendation from heaven, we see in it the expression of:

1. THE LOVING DEVOTION OF JESUS

"This is My beloved Son [or the Son of my love]" (Matt. 3:17). All true love is reciprocal. Because Jesus loved his Father with all his heart, soul, mind, and strength, God said, "My beloved Son." What a challenge this is to us! We can never claim a responsiveness of devotion unless it is genuinely born of love to God.

2. THE PLEASING DEVOTION TO JESUS

"This is my beloved Son, in whom I am well pleased" (Matt. 3:17). The Greek reads: "This is my beloved Son in whom I have delight." God was pleased with his Son because the Son always did those things that pleased the Father. He said, "I always do those things that please Him" (John 8:29). Later on, the apostle Paul could write: "For even Christ did not please Himself" (Rom. 15:3).

Heaven's comment on the pleasing devotion of Jesus Christ is even more remarkable when we recall that his life was, to this point, lived in relative seclusion. As far as we know from Scripture, he had never preached a sermon, cleansed a leper, raised the sick, calmed the seas, calmed the wind, or broken bread to feed the hungry. His life up until now was lived in the intimacy of the home and the activity of a carpenter's workshop. But right in this context he pleased his Father, and God could say, "This is my beloved Son, in whom I am well pleased" (Matt. 3:17).

II. The Delights of Obedience

"Then Jesus, when He had been baptized, came up immediately from the water; and behold, the heavens were opened to Him, and He saw the Spirit of God descending like a dove and alighting upon Him. And suddenly a voice came from heaven, saying, 'This is My beloved Son, in whom I am well pleased'" (Matt. 3:16–17). Here in the language of beautiful symbolism we have three blessings flowing from the life of obedience:

A. The Blessing of the Throne of God

"Behold, the heavens were opened to Him" (Matt. 3:16). The first thing visible when the heaven is open is the throne. John the seer tells us in the Book of Revelation: "After these things I looked, and behold, a door standing open in heaven. . . . And behold, a throne . . ." (Rev. 4:1–2). For the believer, this is the throne of grace where "we may obtain mercy and find grace to help in time of need" (Heb. 4:16). How significant it was that as Jesus came out of the waters of baptism "He prayed [and] the heaven was opened" (Luke 3:21). An open heaven and a throne of grace are the delights of an obedient life.

Do you know the blessing of unbroken fellowship with an enthroned Lord? Is your life lived moment by moment under an open heaven?

B. The Blessing of the Spirit of God

"The Spirit of God descending like a dove . . ." (Matt. 3:16). Here is the second blessing which issues from a life of obedience: the filling and anointing of the Spirit of the living God. When the apostles were put on trial, Peter testified that God gives the Holy Spirit to those who obey him (see Acts 5:32).

The Lord Jesus was full of the Holy Spirit from his mother's womb. There was never a time in those first 30 years when he was not consciously filled with the Holy Spirit. Yet, it was not until his public baptism that he was anointed by that same Spirit for the ministry that lay ahead of him.

The dove-like character of the Holy Spirit represents the requisites for effective service. Bound up in the symbolism of the dove is the thought of sacrifice, humility, peace, and fruitfulness. God grants these to those who trust and obey.

C. The Blessing of the Word of God

"And suddenly a voice came from heaven" (Matt. 3:17). God only speaks to those who obey. Jesus put it this way: "If anyone wants to do His will, he shall know concerning the doctrine, whether it is from God or whether I speak on My own authority" (John 7:17). Revelation and obedience are like two parallel lines. God only reveals while we obey.

> Light received bringeth light,
> Light rejected bringeth night.

If the voice of God is to be heard day by day through the word and prayer, then there must be willing, worthy, and wholehearted obedience.

Illustration

Merrilee had been a Christian long enough to know that sexual immorality was wrong. But she was curious—and impatient. She began the rationalizing process to convince herself that it would be all right. "Just a casual one-night affair won't hurt the other person. A lot of people are used to that sort of thing. If any problems arise, there are plenty of clinics where a person can remain anonymous and be treated. No one needs to know, so my example won't be a stumbling block." On and on she reasoned over a number of weeks. Finally Merrilee had convinced herself that she could "get away with it." One evening she saw a nice looking young man, and she flung a challenge to God: "So, why shouldn't I?" To her surprise an answer came back immediately: "Because I asked you not to." Her prior commitment to be *obedient* to God caused her to see the fallacy of her "logic."[3]

Conclusion

We have seen what constitutes the blessing of obedience: first, the demands, and then, the delights. More than anything else, God make us men and women who are characterized by this great spiritual priority of obedience.

Missions Sunday: The Whole Word to the Whole World
Mark 16:14–20

"Go into all the world and preach the gospel to every creature" (16:15).

Introduction

It is generally accepted that the last twelve verses of Mark 16 are not found in the best manuscripts, thereby presenting one of the major textual problems of the New Testament. The acknowledgment of this omission does not invalidate their genuineness. Dr. G. Campbell Morgan says that "while recognizing the difficulties, . . . I most strongly hold that they are certainly genuine, the weight of evidence both external and internal compelling me to that conclusion." Whatever might be said of these verses cannot alter the truth they teach, inasmuch as the same worldwide commission and its implications are clearly taught elsewhere in the New Testament (see Matt. 28:18–20; Luke 24:46–50; Acts 1:8). Here is set forth:

I. The Missionary Tasks That We Must Accept

"Go into all the world and preach the gospel to every creature" (16:15). When these words were first spoken they were addressed to a mere handful of people; yet Jesus expected them—and every generation since—to reach the whole world with the whole Word. His authoritative utterance was from the captain to the soldier, from the master to the servant, from the Redeemer to the redeemed, from the King to the subject. He did not discuss the possibility of danger, failure, or results. His word was, "Go into all the world and preach the gospel to every creature" (16:15). He knew that great oceans, high mountains, wide deserts, shipwrecks, fever, starvation, and death lay in the path of obedience but, notwithstanding this, he said, "Go." The missionary tasks were:

A. To Reach the Whole World

"Go into all the world" (16:15). Dr. Alexander Maclaren calls this "the divine audacity of Christianity." A study of the commission, as it appears in other parts of the New Testament, makes it clear that the Lord Jesus literally meant all the world—*every country of the world.* Acts 1:8 reminds us that we are to go to "the end of the earth." No country is to be left out, however closed to missionary penetration by the Iron and/or Bamboo Curtain, or anything else.

We are to reach *every culture of the world*—"Go therefore and make disciples of all the nations, baptizing them in the name of the Father and of the Son and of the Holy Spirit, teaching them to observe all things that I have commanded you" (Matt. 28:19–20). We are living in a day of emerging nations. Never before in history has such emphasis been placed upon the dignity, unity, and sovereignty of individual nations. Great importance is also attached to the culture of these nations, and because of this, Christianity is often rejected since it is associated with Western culture. But notwithstanding these difficulties, the commission is to go to every nation.

What is more, we are to reach *every culture of the world*—"Go into all the world and preach the gospel to every creature" (16:15). God is no respecter of persons; therefore man, whatever his color, class, or creed, must be reached with this glorious message of full salvation. When the Lord Jesus uttered these words, the world was not as accessible to the missionary as it is today. But we have no excuse now.

Some years ago the president of the Royal Geographical Society chose a startling phrase to describe the modern world. He said, "Time and distance have now been annihilated by modern inventions and have caused *a shrinkage of the globe.*" We have radio, television, computers, astonishing advances in literacy, and available literature.

Having said this, however, we must hang our heads in shame when we consider that there are millions of people who have never heard the gospel of our Lord Jesus Christ. It has been estimated that "if all the unsaved people in the world were to line up single file at your front door, the line would reach around the world thirty times. And what's worse, this line would grow at the rate of twenty miles per day! If you should drive fifty miles an hour, ten hours a day, it would take you four years and forty days to get to the end of the line, and by the time you reached it, it would have become thirty thousand miles long."[1] How urgent and solemn, then, is this word of commission to go into all the world.

B. To Preach the Whole Word

"Go into all the world and preach the gospel to every creature" (16:15). When Paul defines the gospel, he relates it to the whole Word of God. He writes: "I declare to you the gospel . . . that Christ died for our sins according to the Scriptures, and that He was buried, and that He rose again the third day according to the Scriptures" (1 Cor. 15:1, 3–4). When the same apostle said farewell to the elders and believers at Ephesus, he looked into their faces and said, "I testify to you this day that I am innocent of the blood of all men. For I have not shunned to declare to you the whole counsel of God" (Acts 20:26–27).

No missionary has the right to call himself a Christian, and no Christian has the right to call himself a missionary who has not adopted the same attitude to the task of preaching the Word to the whole world. For too long we have imagined that the sharing of the message of life is relegated to a certain favored few, but this is heresy. Every living Christian is a preacher, every prayerful, earnest godly life is a sermon. There are hundreds of ways of preaching Jesus without standing in the pulpit.

Illustration

A man on his way to prayer meeting one evening saw a stranger looking thoughtfully into an open window of the church. Sensing the leading of the Holy Spirit, the Christian smiled and tactfully invited the man to attend the service with him. The stranger agreed, and it was the beginning of a new life for him, for that night he was saved.[2]

The Holy Scriptures were not given us to simply study objectively, academically, and critically, but rather to love, learn, and live. We cannot dodge the pointedness of the Savior's words when he says, "Preach the gospel to every creature" (16:15).

Illustration

A colporteur [religious book salesman] in North India told the Christmas story, and then read it from the Scriptures. One asked, "How long has it been since God's Son was born into the world?" "About two thousand years," was the missionary's reply. "Then," asked the villager, "who has been hiding this Book all the time?" That is it—hiding the Book. For, after all, is not our keeping the Book from those who need it the same as hiding it? What guilt! You owe it to your Lord and to your world to preach the gospel to every creature.[3]

II. The Missionary Terms That We Must Announce

"He who believes and is baptized will be saved; but he who does not believe will be condemned" (16:16). Nothing could be clearer. If Christ is the subject of our gospel then the terms are:

A. Commitment to Christ

"He who believes . . . will be saved" (16:16). How hopelessly we have failed in clearly announcing the terms of the gospel. The emphasis nowadays is on joining a church, submitting to ordinances, or subscribing to a doctrinal statement; but Jesus said, "He who believes . . . will be saved" (16:16). The terms he laid down are those of a personal relationship to a living Savior and Lord. We miss the point altogether in our preaching if we are not bringing men and women *to* Christ and then building them up *in* Christ.

B. Confession of Christ

"He who believes and is baptized will be saved; but he who does not believe will be condemned" (16:16). Believing *decides* the fact of salvation; baptism *declares* the fact of salvation. Secret discipleship was unknown in the early church. On the day of Pentecost, "those who gladly received his word were baptized; and that day about three thousand souls were added to them" (Acts 2:41). This was not only true of the three thousand, but also of individual conversions described throughout the Acts of the Apostles. Confession of faith was the outward expression of identification with

Christ in his death, burial, and resurrection. It was a declaration of discipleship; it was an open stand of allegiance and obedience. Paul therefore writes to the Jews who had every reason to fear the consequences of open confession and says, "If you confess with your mouth the Lord Jesus and believe in your heart that God has raised Him from the dead, you will be saved" (Rom. 10:9). These terms have never been rescinded, and we fail in our duty not to announce them clearly and categorically.

Illustration

An influential Chinese man who held high office in the educational life of China accepted Christ. He had magnificent prospects before him: position, influence, opportunity, all were his. The study of the New Testament brought him to the conviction that Christ was the Savior of men, and his Savior. After a period of struggle and of counting the cost, he determined to confess Christ before men. His dearest friend pleaded with him not to do so. Then he urged him to secret discipleship. "Bow to the table of Confucius; it is only an empty form, and you can believe what you like in your heart." The official replied, "A few days ago One came to live within my heart. He has changed all life for me forever. I dare not bow to any other, lest he depart."[4]

III. The Missionary Tests That We Must Apply

"And they went out and preached everywhere, the Lord working with them and confirming the word through the accompanying signs" (16:20). "Signs," in the New Testament, are always the evidence of the Savior's presence and power. It follows that if our work of evangelism at home or abroad is to fulfill God's purpose then there must be "signs following." From the passage before us we learn of a twofold test which must be applied to all our missionary endeavor:

A. The Confirmation of the Lord's Presence

"They went out and preached everywhere, the Lord working with them and confirming the word through the accompanying signs" (16:20). The evidence of the Lord's presence is always accompanied by preaching which is authoritative, living, and relevant. When Jesus spoke to men and women, he always called for a verdict. As a result, "the people were astonished at His teaching, for He taught them as one having authority, and not as the scribes" (Matt. 7:28–29). He could say, "The words that I speak to you are spirit, and they are life" (John 6:63). That same Lord indwells us and speaks through us. It follows that if his presence is realized there will be the same confirmation of the Word with "signs following."

B. The Demonstration of the Lord's Power

"And these signs will follow those who believe: In My name they will cast out demons; they will speak with new tongues; they will take up serpents; and if they drink anything deadly, it will by no means hurt them; they will lay hands on the sick, and they will recover" (16:17–18). While it is true that many of the miracles mentioned here were associated, and in a measure restricted, to apostolic power and authority, we cannot and dare not limit the holy one of Israel. Pentecost was not just a day of twenty-four hours; Pentecost is the age of the church, and, therefore, the Holy Spirit is as powerful today as he was when the church was born. As missionaries and evangelists, we must never be satisfied with anything less than a clear demonstration of the Lord's power, through the Holy Spirit, in all we seek to do.

Illustration

Tomahawks in hand, the Indians crept toward the strange tent. As they cautiously peered under the flap, their intention to kill was forgotten. There, in the center of the tent, was a man on his knees. As he prayed, a rattlesnake crossed his feet and paused to strike. But the snake did not strike. It lowered its head again and glided out of the tent. The Indians forever after looked upon David Brainerd as a messenger from the great spirit. Be it ours to learn that in all good work the protection of God is with the worker.[5]

In the release of this power we must expect:

1. VICTORY OVER THE DEVICES OF SATAN

"In My name they will cast out demons" (16:17). We have the right—and, indeed, the authority—in the name of the Lord Jesus and by the power of the Holy Spirit to rebuke Satan. The apostle James exhorts us to "submit to God. Resist the devil and he will flee from [us]" (James 4:7). How often in our work for God we allow the devil to take advantage of us, instead of casting him out in the all-prevailing name of the Son of God.

Illustration

At the age of 17 Stephen Olford was on a trek with his brothers and parents to an African tribe that had never heard the gospel. One day they watched a man go through a witchcraft routine. As he chanted his incantations he became almost demented. Stephen's brother accidentally kicked over one of the idols, and the man became so enraged that he dashed into the forest. Later he emerged, plunged into the fire that was burning in the clearing, picked up the red-hot logs, and flung them up into the air. As they came down they struck his body so that his flesh sizzled. Men came and tried to hold him down, to no avail. Young Olford ran to get his father—a man of God who knew the power of prayer. Taking in the situation at a glance, he commanded the demons in the man to be cast out. Instantly the man collapsed like a punctured balloon, begging for mercy. Fred Olford knelt beside him and very quietly talked to him about Christ, and asked him to receive the Lord into his life, which he did. For three days they remained in that village, while Mrs. Olford washed his wounds, administered medication, and counseled him how to go on in the Christian life. That man became one of the greatest saints in the local assembly and a witness to the heathen around him.

2. Victory Over the Difficulties of Speaking

"They will speak with new tongues" (16:17). Thank God for the excellent achievements of Dr. Frank Laubach and his method of learning a new language. We are indebted also to such organizations as the Wycliffe Bible Translators, and others. So often we forget that behind all these means we have the Holy Spirit who is the Lord of all languages. The history of missions gives plenty of proof of the way the Holy Spirit has enabled the most unlikely individuals to learn what seemed to be impossible languages.

3. Victory Over the Dangers of Sickness

"They will take up serpents; and if they drink anything deadly, it will by no means hurt them; they will lay hands on the sick, and they will recover" (16:18). This is not an invitation to flirt with poisonous snakes or experiment with deadly liquids and infectious diseases; on the contrary, it is a word of instruction concerning the power of the name of Jesus to heal—if and when that is God's will. The doctrine of divine healing is clearly taught in James 5, where we are told that "the prayer of faith will save the sick" (v. 15).

Illustration

In 1540 Martin Luther's great friend and assistant, Frederick Myconius, became sick and was expected to die. On his bed he wrote Luther a loving farewell. Immediately, Luther sent back a reply: "I command thee in the name of God to live, because I still have need of thee in the work of reforming the church. . . . The Lord will never let me hear that thou art dead, but will permit thee to survive me. For this I am praying, this is my will, and may my will be done, because I seek only to glorify the name of God." In a short time Myconius, who had already lost the ability to speak when Luther's letter came, revived. He recovered completely, and lived six more years to survive Luther by two months.[6]

4. Victory over the Darkness of Sin

"And they went out and preached everywhere" (16:20). Wherever man is found without the grace of God there the darkness of sin prevails; and what happened to the first disciples can take place today. If we know the power of our triumphant Lord we can conquer the devices of Satan, the difficulties of speaking, the dangers of sickness, and the darkness of sin. All we have to do is to go in obedience and Jesus promises his presence and power.

Conclusion

We have seen the tasks that we are to accept, the terms that we are to announce, and the tests we are to apply. Dare we fail our Lord in such a desperate hour of the world's history? May the answer from each yielded heart be, "Lord, count on me. Here I am; send me."

Youth Sunday:
The Mind of Youth
Ecclesiastes 11:9–12:7

"Remember now your Creator in the days of your youth, before the difficult days come, and the years draw near when you say, 'I have no pleasure in them'" (12:1).

Introduction

With these words the wise man invites youth to think about God, to remember his Creator. He insists that the time to do this thinking is now. Moses also saw the wisdom of knowing God in youthful days and prayed, "Oh, satisfy us early with Your mercy, that we may rejoice and be glad all our days!" (Ps. 90:14). Never was there such a need for inculcating youth with thoughts about God as today. Only as they make him a vital part of their lives will there be hope for the civilization of tomorrow. Three questions should be asked by every young person:

I. What Shall I Think of My Creator?

"Remember now *your* Creator" (12:1). The word "your" is our key here. It carries the idea of correspondence between the Creator and the creature and suggests that if youth would learn of its Creator they must examine the measure of his likeness in their lives. The Bible encourages such an examination for it declares that "God created man in His own image; in the image of God He created him" (Gen. 1:27). This takes three forms:

A. The Spirit

"He has made everything beautiful in its time. . . . He has put eternity in their hearts" (Eccles. 3:11). This is the inherent spirit-consciousness that makes us aware of God. Somebody has called it "the vast capacity for God or the vast emptiness without him." By the law of correspondence we learn that our Creator is also spirit. Jesus declared, "God is Spirit, and those who worship Him must worship in spirit and truth" (John 4:24).

Illustration

During his student days, Stephen Olford studied the subject of anthropology. What impressed him most was the fact that wherever man is found—however primitive—he is basically religious. No wonder the Bible says, "He has put eternity in" man's heart (Eccles. 3:11). This is why people in the bush of Africa still worship the great spirit, offering blood sacrifices and peace offerings in order to gain favor. Most have never heard of the Bible or of Jesus Christ the Savior, but they are religious.

B. The Soul

"The spirit will return to God who gave it" (12:7); and again: "The LORD God formed man . . . and breathed into his nostrils the breath of life" (Gen. 2:7). That is our self-consciousness with a capacity to think, love, and act; in a word, *personality.* This suggests that our Creator must be the infinite personality with an all-knowing mind, an all-loving heart, and an all-powerful will. An intelligent understanding of this correspondence between the Creator and the creature should call from us a faith in the God who exists and rewards all those who diligently seek him.

C. The Body

"The dust will return to the earth as it was" (12:7). When Paul speaks of man as a tripartite being, he prays: "May your whole spirit, soul, and body be preserved blameless at the coming of our Lord Jesus Christ" (1 Thess. 5:23). This is our sense-consciousness. It is the vehicle through which our personality is expressed. Even in this respect we can learn of our Creator because there came a point in time when, for the purpose of expressing himself in terms which you and I could understand, the Creator became flesh and appeared in the likeness of men. John puts it beautifully when he says, "The Word became flesh and dwelt among us, and we beheld His glory, the glory as of the only begotten of the Father, full of grace and truth" (John 1:14); and then he adds: "No one has seen God at any time. The only begotten Son, who is in the bosom of the Father, He has declared Him" (John 1:18). This is why the Lord Jesus could say, "He who has seen Me has seen the Father" (John 14:9).

So in answer to the question, "What shall I think of my Creator?" we have to state that the Creator is the spiritual and personal God "who at various times and in different ways spoke in time past to the fathers by the prophets; [but] has in these last days spoken to us by His Son [the Christ of history]" (Heb. 1:1–2).

II. Why Shall I Think of My Creator?

"*Remember* now your *Creator*" (12:1). In asking the question "Why?" we are thinking of three aspects of the Creator's almighty power. There is:

A. God's Creative Power

"For by Him all things were created" (Col. 1:16). This includes the universe around us as well as the universe within us. As the psalmist contemplated the world around him he wrote: "The heavens declare the glory of God; and the firmament shows His handiwork" (Ps. 19:1); and when he examined the world within him he had to exclaim, "I am fearfully and wonderfully made" (Ps. 139:14). Behind our parents and secondary causes is the hand of the Almighty, to whom we owe our very existence.

This is an aspect of truth which is largely forgotten today. In the technological climate in which we are educated we tend to think of ourselves as cogs in a machine, rather than unique and scintillating personalities. It is both a biblical and physical fact that God never makes duplicates; he always makes originals. There is only one *you and me.* Have we ever knelt in God's presence and thanked him for making us just as we are—special people? Therefore, we need to develop the art, by the power of Christ, to live with the person he made, instead of comparing ourselves with others. God has made us for himself, and we constitute a facet of the diamond of his glorious handiwork from which light can be reflected in a way it couldn't be from anyone else. To understand this fully is to bow in worship before our Creator God. It should change our whole conception of the importance of our spirits, souls, and bodies. How can anyone deaden his spirit, destroy his soul, or defile his body, if he understands the nature and origin of his being? God has a purpose for our lives and he is the only one who can give fulfillment and meaning.

Illustration

It is one of the marvels of nature that of all the five billion faces in the world no two are exactly alike. There are, of course, resemblances, similarities, likenesses, but, strictly speaking, there is no such thing as a "double." Not even what we call "identical twins" are precisely the same. Each face is unique. God breaks the mold after making every individual human countenance. If, as the scientists tell us, no two leaves or snowflakes are identical, surely it ought not to be too hard for us to believe in a similar vast variation of the human visage; and we might add, personality.[1]

B. God's Redemptive Power

According to Peter, our God is "a faithful Creator" (1 Peter 4:19). Were it not for his faithfulness and mercy we would be consumed. It is only because of his providence, protection, and provision that we continue to "live and move and have our being" (Acts 17:28). There are individuals who can recall the times they faced imminent danger, yet were spared. The Bible declares that behind every life are both evil spirits and guardian angels (see Eph. 6:12; Ps. 91:11). Such messengers of protection are "sent forth to minister for those who will inherit salvation" (Heb. 1:14). More important than the protective power of God is his redemptive power. In the larger context of Peter's reference to God as "a faithful Creator" (1 Peter 4:19) is that glorious statement concerning our reconciliation to God through the death of Christ our God. He states: "If the righteous one is scarcely saved, where will the ungodly and the sinner appear?" (1 Peter 4:18). Because he is a faithful Creator he is a faithful Redeemer.

C. God's Possessive Power

He says, "I am the LORD, your Holy One, the Creator of Israel, your King" (Isa. 43:15). As Creator and King, he claims unlimited sway over our spirits, souls, and bodies. Therefore:

> Make Jesus King, thro' Him we shall live;
> Our souls and our bodies to Him let us give;

His praises we'll sing, and others we'll bring,
Till the whole of creation shall make Jesus King.

                            J. Russell Darbyshire

There is only one answer to that poetical question, "You are worthy, O Lord, to receive glory and honor and power; for You created all things, and by Your will they exist and were created" (Rev. 4:11).

III. When Shall I Think of My Creator?

"Remember now your Creator" (12:1). This is further amplified in the verse: "now . . . in the days of your youth, before the difficult days come, and the years draw near when you say, 'I have no pleasure in them'" (12:1). These statements combine to teach that the time for a youth to think of his Creator is during the period of:

A. *Youthful Impressions*

"Now . . . in the days of your youth" (12:1). Youth is a time for early impressions. It has been said that earliest impressions are longest impressions. When the Lord Jesus endeavored to teach the lessons of humility and teachability, he took a little child in his arms and said, "Unless you are converted and become as little children, you will by no means enter the kingdom of heaven" (Matt. 18:3).

Illustration

Stephen Olford recalls that the deepest impressions upon his life date back to his boyhood days in Africa. As the son of missionary parents, he knew what it was to camp and trek for weeks on end. His father would lead family worship at dawn, and then conduct a Bible study at dusk. One particular series he remembers was on the tabernacle in the wilderness. To this day he can still visualize the scene outside their tent, as he sat with African carriers around the campfire, listening with rapt attention to the expositions of divine truth. The missionary's tent served to represent the tabernacle in the wilderness, the fire the brazen altar, and a canvass washbasin the laver. Those memories never left him, mainly because they were youthful impressions.

B. Youthful Innocence

"Before the difficult days come . . . , " says Solomon (12:1). While everyone is born in sin, it must be conceded that youth is the period of comparative innocence. It is a time to teach the mind that has not been poisoned, gain the ear that has not been deafened, win the heart that has not been hardened, and control the will that has not been taken captive.

All of us can remember our younger days, when the death of our favorite pet brought tears to our eyes; but now we are unmoved by the tragedy we see on television or hear over radio. We have failed to pray for unconverted friends and relatives, much less wept for their souls!

C. Youthful Interests

Solomon continues, "Remember now your Creator . . . before the difficult days come, and the years draw near when you say, 'I have no pleasure in them'" (12:1). Someone has said, "If I am to be interested in anything speak to me when I'm young." Old age can be the enemy of interest. The challenge of life makes little appeal to old people. The time to think of your Creator is now, in the days of youthful impressions, youthful innocence, and youthful interests.

Dr. Vance Havner used to deliver a sermon entitled "Have You Lost the Wonder?" His text was the one already referred to (Matt. 18:3)—"Unless you are converted and become as little children, you will by no means enter the kingdom of heaven." He would describe the wonder that fills the eyes, mind, and heart of a little child who is being shown around a garden or a toy shop. He then would go on to show how easily we can become deadened to the wonders of our Creator God. Do we still enjoy the song of the bird, the glow of a sunset, the beauty of a snowflake, the sound of pounding surf, the laughter of little children? Oh, that God would ever keep us young in heart, even though we inevitably advance in age!

Conclusion

To sum up, ask and answer those questions again:
1Q. What shall I think of my Creator?
1A. He is my God and Savior.
2Q. Why shall I think of my Creator?
2A. He claims my all.
3Q. When shall I think of my Creator?
3A. Now, while I am young.

May your response be:

>   His, by reason of creation,
>   His, He paid the price for me;
>   His, by the life-giving Spirit,
>   His, because I want to be.
>   Stephen F. Olford

Youth Sunday:
The Way of Youth
Psalm 119:9

"How can a young man cleanse his way? By taking heed according to Your word" (119:9).

Introduction

Scholars maintain that David wrote Psalm 119 because it breathes the language of the sweet singer of Israel. He knew what it was to be a shepherd boy on the Bethlehem fields with his sling, with his sheep, and with his God. Undoubtedly, it was during these early years that he learned that if his life were to be pure, clean, and noble, he must know the truth that is embodied in our text. Here we have spelled out for us:

I. The Essential Problem of Youth

"How can a young man cleanse his way? By taking heed according to Your word" (Ps. 119:9). The fact that cleansing is mentioned presupposes defilement; and defilement, in turn, presupposes the basic problem of every boy and girl, man and woman. It is twofold:

A. The Presence of Sin in the Life

"For all have sinned and fall short of the glory of God" (Rom. 3:23). Only a fool would deny the fact that present in the youngest child or the oldest person is a principle that drives an individual to sin and defeat. The two words "young man" are best translated by the term "youth," and therefore apply to a girl as well as a fellow.

That prince of expositors, Dr. G. Campbell Morgan once expounded this text. He pointed out that the Hebrew word for "young man" or "youth" is derived from a root which means "the mane of a lion." If you know anything about the life and habitat of this monarch of the forest you will know that when the lion is at rest his mane will flop from one side to the other. In a hostile situation the lion's mane will stand erect; in deadly conflict his mane will be splattered with blood. That is a picture of youth. Their ups and downs can be likened to the mane of a lion.

We see then that the basic problem of the human race is the presence of sin in the life. Little children look so innocent when they are sound asleep, but deep within their hearts is the presence of sin. The Bible says that we are brought forth in iniquity and conceived in sin (see Ps. 51:5). From the very beginning of life there is a bias to sin. The Bible reminds us: "Therefore, just as through one man sin entered the world, and death through sin, . . . thus death spread to all men, because all sinned" (Rom. 5:12).

Illustration

Many years ago three scientists working for the University of Melbourne, capital of Victoria in Australia, invented a tiny television camera that could be swallowed by a patient under examination. It would then flash clear pictures on an enlarged screen so that the internal organs, their condition and activities, could be accurately seen. Hailed as one of the greatest advances in medicine and surgery, its pictures, magnified 30-40 times on a television screen, allows doctors to completely observe heretofore hidden cavities. Doctors now are able to observe what is taking place inside the patient. Science hails this as a great discovery, but it is nothing new. God's great camera, the Bible, illuminated by the Holy Spirit, has long ago given us a picture of our insides, not only the stomach, but the "heart." He even sees our thoughts (see Ps. 139:2). What does God's camera reveal in the natural heart? Only filth, deceitfulness, and sin (see Ps. 14:3; Jer. 17:9; Rom. 5:12). But God's camera also provides the cure: "He who hears My word and believes in Him who sent Me has everlasting life" (John 5:24).[1]

B. The Practice of Sin in the Life

"Whoever commits sin is a slave of sin" (John 8:34). This history of sin follows a prescribed pattern:

1. THERE IS THE DELIGHT OF SIN

The Bible speaks of "the passing pleasures of sin" (Heb. 11:25). The devil sees to it that every appearance of sin is either glamorized or rationalized.

2. THERE IS THE DEFILEMENT OF SIN

"Out of the heart proceed . . . the things which defile a man" (Matt. 15:19–20). Sinful thoughts are followed by sinful words, and then sinful deeds, until the whole life is defiled.

3. THERE IS THE DEFEAT OF SIN

Paul says: "For the good that I will to do, I do not do; but the evil I will not to do, that I practice. Now if I do what I will not to do, it is no longer I who do it, but sin that dwells in me" (Rom. 7:19–20). Sin takes hold of our lives. We struggle in vain to do good. At last we give up in despair, crying, "O wretched man that I am! Who will deliver me from this body of death?" (Rom. 7:24).

4. THERE IS THE DESTRUCTION OF SIN

"The wages of sin is death" (Rom. 6:23); "The soul who sins shall die" (Ezek. 18:4); "Sin, when it is fullgrown, brings forth death" (James 1:15). This is the ultimate result of a life of sin. Death is not only the separation of the spirit from the body, but the soul from God.

Illustration

A young man got into the habit of eating six pizzas at one sitting and finishing off a case of beer while watching television in his father's tavern. His doctor warned him that his weight was endangering his life, but he failed to listen. Within two months, this five-foot-ten-inch young man was killed by a heart attack. At the time of his death he weighed 650 pounds. Six men were needed to carry his body to a hearse after he was pronounced dead. How true the Bible is when it says, "Whatever a man sows, that he will also reap. For he who sows to his flesh will of the flesh reap corruption" (Gal. 6:7–8). There is such a thing as the destruction of sin.

II. The Effectual Answer to Youth

"How can a young man cleanse his way? By taking heed according to Your word" (119:9). These words of David mean at least two things; first:

A. Hearing the Word

"Taking heed *according to Your word*" (119:9). God has spoken to men and women, young and old, in his Son Jesus Christ. Hebrews 1:1 puts it this way: "God, who at various times and in different ways spoke in time past to the fathers by the prophets, has in these last days spoken to us by His Son" As Professor Emil Brunner has put it: "Jesus Christ is God's conversation with men." God has broken into time in the inescapable Christ of history. The Son of God has taken the sins of youth and old age to the cross and nailed them there forever. He has conquered death and emerged as the mighty, victorious Lord who wants to enter the heart of every young person who hears his voice. Indeed, he says, "Behold, I stand at the door and knock. If anyone hears My voice and opens the door, I will come in to him and dine with him, and he with Me" (Rev. 3:20). People who try to change their lives from the outside are fooling themselves. Only God can change the life, and this begins when Christ comes into the heart through the hearing of the Word. The Word is not only the written Word, it is the spoken Word, in terms of flesh and blood as revealed in the person of Jesus Christ.

B. Heeding the Word

"By taking *heed* according to Your word" (119:9). Are we prepared to act upon this word of the gospel? Are we prepared to hear and to heed the voice of the Son of God and live? Remember that the Bible says we are to be "doers of the word, and not hearers only, deceiving [ourselves]" (James 1:22). There are thousands of people who hear religious sermons from the pulpit, over radio and TV, but do nothing about it. God has not promised any cleansing or change of life until there is obedience to the word of the gospel. Heed the Word and something will happen! There will be:

1. Salvation

The apostle speaks of "the Holy Scriptures, which are able to make you wise for salvation through faith which is in Christ Jesus" (2 Tim. 3:15); and again: "Faith comes by hearing, and hearing by the word of

God" (Rom. 10:17). Saving faith is dependent upon the hearing and heeding of the gospel of Jesus Christ.

2. SANCTIFICATION

Thinking of his disciples in all ages, Jesus prayed, "Sanctify them by Your truth. Your word is truth" (John 17:17).

Stephen Olford met a naval officer during World War II and asked him if he were a Christian. He said that he was, and then told how it had come about. He had been a Cambridge undergraduate, a member of an atheistic organization in which he took great delight in debating against Christianity. Then he was called to join the Navy, and from day one he was miserable. Facing life in the raw, all sense of security had left him.

To make things worse, he shared a bunk with a radiant Christian fellow who knew his Bible and his God. One day, after fierce action from overhead bombers, he sought seclusion in his bunk. The vivid scenes of wounded and dying men were still fresh in his mind. Depressed and overcome with fear, he picked up his mate's Bible and opened it. For the first time in his life he prayed, "O God, if you exist, speak to me from this Book." The Bible opened at the Gospel of John, and as he perused the pages the Spirit of God revealed the reality of the saving Christ. Relating the story to Stephen Olford, he exclaimed, "It was as if I could see him with the eyes of my heart, and I prayed, 'Jesus Christ, thou Son of God, come into my life and save me' and the miracle happened."

Olford, who at the time was an Army Scripture Reader, asked him, "Have all your intellectual difficulties been solved?" "Quite honestly," he replied, "not all of them, but I believe that the God who solved some of them will complete the work as I mature in the Christian life." Then Mr. Olford asked him an important question: "What do you consider to be the greatest argument for the authority and infallibility of the Bible?" The naval officer answered, "I believe this to be the Bible because the more I read it, the more pure and holy I become."

Yes, to hear and to heed the Word of God is not only to be saved, but to be sanctified.

3. Satisfaction

Jeremiah says, "Your words were found, and I ate them, and Your word was to me the joy and rejoicing of my heart" (Jer. 15:16). Nothing is more satisfying than the full-orbed truth of God's Word that quickens our spirits, that informs our minds, that strengthens our hearts, that liberates our wills and purifies our bodies. Indeed, the answer to juvenile delinquency in our world today is Jesus Christ, the mighty Savior, who is revealed to us in this wonderful Book.

4. Service

"All Scripture is given by inspiration of God, and is profitable for doctrine, for reproof, for correction, for instruction in righteousness, that the man of God may be complete, thoroughly equipped for every good work" (2 Tim. 3:16–17). No one can heed the doctrine, reproof, correction, and instruction in righteousness without becoming a man of God, thoroughly equipped for every good work. Vocational orientation is one of the products of a life that conforms to the will of God.

Illustration

As a boy he missed out on a common education, but was converted to God and turned to the Bible for daily reading. He learned ambition from the Bible and assayed tasks that seemed beyond his ability and came to a place of power and influence such as has been granted to few persons of this generation. Asked about his life-work, he said, "I have no native ability beyond the ordinary, but I have found in God's Word the power that enables the commonplace man to do the uncommon things for an everlasting God."

Conclusion

We have seen what constitutes the essential problem of youth and the effectual answer to youth. We have asked the question, "How can a young man cleanse his way?" and we have answered it by saying, "by taking heed according to Your word" (119:9). Are you prepared to hear and heed God's Word, even the message of the gospel, and come into a life of salvation, sanctification, satisfaction, and service? If so, make these words your prayer:

> Just as I am, young, strong, and free,
> To be the best that I can be
> For truth, and righteousness and Thee,
> Lord of my life, I come.
>
> Marianne Hearn

Youth Sunday:
The Yoke of Youth
Lamentations 3:22–33

"It is good for a man to bear the yoke in his youth" (3:27).

Introduction

The Lamentations of Jeremiah are one of the most profound and precious disclosures of God's purpose for his people. In chapter after chapter the prophet shows that despite the trials and tears of everyday life God is ever silently planning in love for his own. In the verses before us, Jeremiah recalls the days of his youth and remembers what God put him through before he could be the divine spokesman to his generation. He says, "It is good for a man to bear the yoke in his youth" (3:27)—words not popular in today's society, but necessary to a correct understanding of God's purpose for young life. Observe:

I. The Desirability of the Yoke of Youth

"It is good for a man to bear the yoke in his youth" (3:27). Three times over—in vv. 25, 26, and 27—we have the little word "good," and its meaning is not difficult to follow. Jeremiah had been a young man but now he was old. As he retraces the steps through which God had led him he declares, "It is good for a man to bear the yoke in his youth" (3:27). Jeremiah recalls that the "yoke" for him was God's method of teaching and training him. As someone has put it, "Early discipline begets mature dependability." Then he gives us two reasons for accepting the yoke:

A. God Gives the Yoke

"The LORD is good to those who wait for Him" (3:25). The gifts of God are always desirable because the Word of God says that "No good thing will He withhold from those who walk uprightly" (Ps. 84:11). Jeremiah revels in this fact. He exclaims, "Through the LORD's mercies we are not consumed, because His compassions fail not" (3:22). Were we to receive what we deserve, God would annihilate us before we ever reached manhood. Indeed, he goes on to say that "His compassions . . . are new every morning" (3:22–23), or more literally, "are adapted to every day's requirements." Then he declares, "Great is Your faithfulness" (3:23). To him, the Lord had become his portion (see 3:24); therefore, he had complete confidence in his covenant-keeping God. In the light of this he acknowledges that the yoke of God's provision is not only desirable, but absolutely essential for his life.

The Lord Jesus must have been thinking of these very words when he said, "Come to Me, all you who labor and are heavy laden, and I will give you rest. *Take My yoke upon you* and learn from Me, for I am gentle and lowly in heart, and you will find rest for your souls. For My *yoke is easy* and My burden is light" (Matt. 11:28–30).

Illustration
John T. Fair tells the story of a man who was carrying a heavy basket. His son offered to help him. The father cut a large stick and placed it through the handle of the basket so that the end toward himself was very short, while the end toward the boy was three or four times as long. Each took hold of his end of the stick, and the basket was lifted and carried easily. The son was bearing the burden with the father. He found his work easy and light because his father assumed the heavier end of the load. So it is when we live for Jesus—"Take My yoke upon you, and learn from Me. . . . for My yoke is easy, and My burden is light" (Matt. 11:29–30).[1]

Let us remember this fact when we are tempted to rebel against the yoke. Quite clearly, from the words of our Savior, this yoke of God's provision involves the *invitation* of the gospel—"Come to Me, all you who labor and are heavy laden, and I will give you rest"; then the *obligation* of the gospel—"Take My yoke upon you"; and then finally, the *education* of the gospel—"Learn from Me, for I am gentle, and lowly in heart, and you will find rest for your souls. For My yoke is easy and My burden is light" (Matt. 11:28–30).

B. Man Needs the Yoke

"It is good that one should hope and wait quietly for the salvation of the LORD" (3:26). Without the yoke of God's provision no one—young or old—can ever experience or enjoy the full salvation which God has provided for all who believe. In terms of New Testament language, this yoke implies not only union with Christ, but communion with Christ; not only the fact of salvation but the fullness of salvation. So the yoke of youth is desirable. Are we prepared to accept this yoke of God's purpose for our lives?

II. The Discipline of the Yoke of Youth

"It is good for a man to bear the yoke in youth" (3:27). Undoubtedly, Jeremiah had watched many a farmer as he yoked his oxen to plow the furrows, to draw the water, or to carry the burdens. In his mind, the yoke was essentially an instrument of discipline and is made clear in the verses that follow our text:

A. There Is the Discipline of Silence

"Let him sit alone and keep silent, because God has laid it on him" (3:28), or more literally, "Let him sit alone and keep silence when he [Jehovah] has laid the yoke on him." One of the great problems of youth is that of rebellion against discipline; it is a problem that is found at every stage of life. Jeremiah had to learn that there are times in our lives when we have to accept discipline in silence.

No one demonstrated this more than our wonderful Lord and Savior Jesus Christ. Isaiah tells us that "He was led as a lamb to the slaughter, and as a sheep before its shearers is silent, so He opened not His mouth" (Isa. 53:7). Peter reminds us that "when He was reviled, [he] did not revile in return; when He suffered, He did not threaten, but committed Himself to Him who judges righteously" (1 Peter 2:23). Then there was that occasion when, standing before Pilate, "He answered him not one word, so that the governor marveled greatly" (Matt. 27:14). When a young person realizes that God is ever and always silently planning for him in love, rebellion ceases and discipline is accepted quietly and obediently.

Amplify

Often the best answer to our critics is to say *nothing* in return. It is much more difficult to learn to keep still than to learn to speak. If the accusation is true, you have no answer; if it is not true, it needs no answer. If you do anything worthwhile, you will be talked about. If no one talks about you, it is a sign you have never done anything worth talking about. Someone has said, "Never mind what they say about you, just so they talk about you." It is a hard lesson to learn, but one most worthwhile—just to answer your slanderers with silence. If someone throws mud at you—wait till it *dries*—and it will just rub off. Don't rub it in while it is wet—give it time to dry. An ancient poet was informed that a malicious enemy with a poisoned tongue was speaking ill about him to *all the world*. The poet answered, "Let him alone, it is better that he speak ill of me to the world, than that *all the world* should speak ill of me to him." Learn to answer your accusers with silence.[2]

B. There Is the Discipline of Submission

"Let him put his mouth in the dust—there may yet be hope" (3:29). This was an Oriental manner of expressing submission. It is a picture of an Eastern subject, prostrate before his king. His face is laid in the dust so that he cannot answer back. How expressive of total submission to the lordship of Jesus Christ. No one can acknowledge Christ as sovereign without accepting his yoke. This calls for submission to the Savior in every area of life. In the home, children are to "obey [their] . . . parents in the Lord" (Eph. 6:1). In the church, young and old are to "obey those who rule over [them]" (Heb. 13:17); and in the world, Peter makes it clear that every Christian is to "submit . . . to every ordinance of man for the Lord's sake" (1 Peter 2:13). Have you ever accepted the yoke of submission? It is a discipline to which Jesus Christ has called us.

C. There Is the Discipline of Suffering

"Let him give his cheek to the one who strikes him, and be full of reproach" (3:30). How this matches up with our Savior's words in the Sermon on the Mount: "Whoever slaps you on your right cheek, turn the other to him also" (Matt. 5:39). This is exactly what Jesus did as he steadfastly set his face to go toward Jerusalem and then on to the cross. Wicked men blindfolded him and struck him with a rod. They plucked the hair from his cheek, they spat in his face; but in all his suffering he never retaliated.

Nothing is more grueling and demanding in a young person's life than to accept the discipline of suffering without retaliation or resentment. This is the way of discipleship. Jesus said, "Whoever does not bear his cross and come after Me cannot be My disciple" (Luke 14:27). The cross not only symbolizes the disciplines of silence and submission, but also of suffering. Until such discipline is accepted gladly and obediently a person is not qualified to serve Jesus Christ.

Illustration

Richard Weaver, a Christian worker, earned his living in the mines. He had the higher priority, however, of trying to bring his associates in contact with the Savior and his soul-restoring Word. While most of the men were indifferent, one became offended by his witness, and finally exclaimed, "I'm sick of your constant preaching. I've a good mind to smack you in the face!" "Go ahead if it will make you feel better," replied Weaver. The man immediately struck him a stinging blow. The Christian did not retaliate but turned the other cheek. Again the unbeliever struck him and then walked away, cursing under his breath. Weaver called after him, "I forgive you, and still pray that the Lord will save you!" The next morning his assailant was waiting for him when he came to work. "Oh, Dick," he said, his voice filled with emotion, "do you really forgive me for what I did yesterday?" "Certainly," said Weaver extending his hand. As he told him again the message of salvation, God opened the man's heart, and he received Christ.[3]

III. The Design of the Yoke of Youth

"It is good for a man to bear the yoke in his youth" (3:27). If this statement is true then, obviously, there is a hidden and holy design in this needful experience of life. The answer is not hard to find. In the concluding words of this section we have the design of God clearly outlined. The yoke of youth is the means by which young and old can experience:

A. The Promise of God for Life

"For the Lord will not cast off forever" (3:31). These words are a quotation from at least two psalms (94:14 and 77:7). Jeremiah in his prophecy uses similar words (see Jer. 3:5, 12). He was confident of one thing: that as long as he was under the yoke God would continue to work until he had perfected that which concerned him (see Ps. 138:8). This is a tremendous thought. As long as we accept the yoke of divine discipline, God will see to it that he brings to pass in our lives all that he has promised to do. This affects not only our character, but our conduct as well; not only our salvation, but our service. Our usefulness to God is proportionate to our yieldedness to him. God only uses yokefellows. David puts it perfectly when he says, "Commit your way to the LORD, trust also in Him, and He shall bring it to pass" (Ps. 37:5). The apostle echoes the same thought in Ephesians 2:10—"We are His workmanship, created in Christ Jesus for good works, which God prepared beforehand that we should walk in them" (Eph. 2:10). Young people, particularly, are concerned about their future careers. There is no need to fret or worry about this as long as they are prepared to accept the yoke of Christ. The promise is clear: "The LORD will not cast off forever" (3:31). It may seem like God has abandoned us, but, in point of fact, he is silently planning for us in love.

B. The Purpose of God for Life

"Though He causes grief, yet He will show compassion according to the multitude of His mercies. For He does not afflict willingly, nor grieve the children of men" (3:32–33). These are precious words indeed!

They reveal that God's purpose for our lives is an increasing understanding of his love. So often we are tempted to complain and even doubt, when undergoing the disciplines of God, but the fact remains that "whom the LORD loves He chastens." The reason for doing this is that we might be "partakers of His holiness" (Heb. 12:6, 10). Such holiness, of course, is conformity "to the image of [God's] . . . Son . . ." (Rom. 8:29). Paul says, "All things work together for good to those who love God, to those who are the called according to His purpose" (Rom. 8:28).

We talk about the grief and affliction through which we pass sometimes, but that is not to be compared with the grief which our heavenly Father experiences. Look at verses 32–33 again: "Though He causes grief, yet He will show compassion according to the multitude of His mercies. For He does not afflict willingly, nor grieve the children of men" (3:32–33). When the surgeon picks up his scalpel to make an incision, he does not willingly desire to hurt or afflict, even though pain is involved; his purpose is to heal and restore.

The divine design in bearing the yoke of youth is not only to prove God's promise in all the wonder of his salvation and service in our lives, but also to prove his purpose of love in making us more and more like his Son—even Jesus Christ our Lord.

Illustration

In the pictures of the ancient Roman method of threshing grain, one man is always seen stirring up the sheaves while another rides over them in a crude cart equipped with rollers instead of wheels. Sharp stones and rough bits of iron were attached to these cylinders to help separate the husks from the grain. This simple cart was called a *tribulum*—from which we get our word "tribulation." When great affliction comes to us, we often think of ourselves as being torn to pieces under the cruel pressures of adverse circumstances. No thresher ever yoked up his *tribulum* for the mere purpose of tearing up his sheaves, but to disclose the precious grain. Similarly, our loving Savior never puts us under the pressures of sorrow and disappointment needlessly.[4]

Conclusion

As long as we live on earth we are, like youth, in a constant process of development and training. Whether we are children, young men, or fathers, we are expected to accept this yoke because it is "good." God gives it and everyone needs it. Let us not chafe or shrink from this yoke, but rather accept it gratefully and wear it obediently.

13

Youth Sunday:
The Gift of Youth
John 6:5-14

"There is a lad here" (6:9).

Introduction

The feeding of the five thousand is a miracle which is recorded by each of the gospel writers. This fact underscores the special importance and the spiritual significance of this happening in the ministry of our Lord. In the events that took place on this memorable occasion we see illustrated the redemptive compassion, provision, and intention of our Savior. There was divine compassion because Jesus would not turn hungry people away. He asked, "Where shall we buy bread, that these may eat?" (6:5). There was divine provision because by his creative power he multiplied five barley loaves and two small fish to feed "five thousand men, besides women and children" (Matt. 14:21). There was divine intention because

Jesus took on an unknown boy and through his instrumentality blessed not only multitudes by the Sea of Galilee, but countless numbers throughout the centuries. It is the story of this little boy which gives this miracle a relevance to your life and mine. Consider three salient lessons that emerge from the story before us:

I. The Availability of the Lad

"There is a lad here" (6:9). Have you ever wondered why that boy was near the Sea of Galilee that day? How is it that he became available at the right time, at the right place, for the right use? The answer is twofold:

A. The Lad Was Willing to Seek Jesus

"There is a lad here" (6:9). The story does not tell us what influenced this boy to follow the crowd in order to see Jesus. He may have had godly parents who encouraged him to seek the master. On the other hand, he may have heard of some wonderful cures which the Savior had performed, and so followed the multitudes in the hope of witnessing further miracles. This is mere speculation. What is clear, though, is the fact that the boy was there just when Jesus needed him, and there was a willingness in his heart to seek the Lord. No one seeks Jesus in this fashion without finding him. Jeremiah 29:13 tells us: "You will seek Me and find Me, when you search for Me with all your heart." What is even more important, the gospel reveals that Jesus came into the world "to seek and to save that which was lost" (Luke 19:10). When a seeking Savior meets a seeking sinner it is the moment of truth. If you are seeking Jesus then you are a candidate for blessing.

B. The Lad Was Waiting to Serve Jesus

"There is a lad here who has five barley loaves and two small fish" (6:9). It is evident from the story that he thought so much of Christ that when he was asked to part with his five loaves and two small fish he was ready to surrender them.

Invariably, this has been true of youth throughout the centuries. The psalmist says, "Your people shall be volunteers in the day of Your power; in the beauties of holiness, from the womb of the morning, You have the dew of Your youth" (Ps. 110:3; see also Eccles. 12:1). One of the reasons God is using young people today is because of their desire to serve. We wrongly judge our present generation if we suggest that they have no concern for the issues of the hour. It can be established that practically every major problem facing the world today is being tackled by young people. Their methods are not always commendable and their zeal is often misdirected, but their desire to serve is unquestionable.

Are we available to Jesus Christ? Are we willing to seek him, and are we waiting to serve him?

Amplify
What is the meaning of life? Is it how long we live, how famous we become, or how rich we are at retirement? Jesus says that the measure of life is in our service, the good we do for others. Out of this spirit has come every Christian college and school, orphanage, and beneficent work in the world. George W. Truett, the great Baptist preacher, said, "It is not the talents one has that makes him great, however many and brilliant they may be; it is not the vast amount of study that gives mental enrichment to the mind and life; it is not in shining social qualities; it is not the large accumulation of wealth that secures peace and honor. In none of these, measured by God's standards, does greatness reside. . . . True greatness consists in the use of all the talents one has in unselfish ministry to others."[1]

II. The Potentiality of the Lad

"There is a lad here who has five barley loaves and two small fish" (6:9). That statement is highly suggestive.

Those five barley loaves represented the poorest fare in any Jewish home. Barley loaves were usually given to donkeys, mules, and other livestock. Only the destitute ate barley loaves, for the staple food was usually made of wheat. Then there were those two small fish, probably caught in the Sea of Galilee, now cooked and shriveled up! This is all the boy had, but what a potential in the hands of the master! How true are the words, "Little is much when God is in it." As we look at this narrative it is obvious that in the five loaves and the two small fish there was:

A. The Potential for Fulfilling the Will of the Master

Jesus said, "Make the people sit down." Later we read he "took the loaves, and when He had given thanks He distributed them to the disciples, and the disciples to those sitting down; and likewise of the fish, as much as they wanted" (6:10–11). The one concern of our Lord was to feed the multitude. Such was his heart of compassion that he could not send them away hungry. In the potential of that lad's lunch he saw more than enough to feed that vast multitude. Indeed, we are told that when they gathered the leftovers it filled twelve baskets! (6:13). There is nothing more wonderful in all the world than fulfilling the will of the master.

B. The Potential for Supplying the Need of the People

"They were [all] filled" (6:12). One boy, five barley loaves, two small fish, and more than five thousand people were satisfied. What a miracle! This is exactly what God does when we are prepared to surrender our all to him.

When our Savior said, "Go into all the world and preach the gospel to every creature" (Mark 16:15) he was not using rhetoric or hyperbole. He meant exactly what he said—"all the world . . . to every creature." The disciples took these words so seriously that the world was evangelized in some thirty years after the day of Pentecost.

The basic need of men and women today is still the saving grace of our Lord Jesus Christ. There is no service that we can render with more urgency and a sense of importance than that of sharing the Bread of Life. Oh, that our response might be, "There is a lad here" (6:9).

C. The Potential for Advancing the Cause of the Gospel

We read that "those men, when they had seen the sign [or miracle] that Jesus did, said, 'This is truly the Prophet who is to come into the world'" (6:14). For two thousand years this story has been told and retold; and because one little boy was willing to sacrifice his lunch the cause of the gospel has been advanced. This incident is of such eternal consequence that God has seen fit to include it in the gospel record. In God's eyes, everything we do for Jesus Christ will abide forever. How true are those words:

> Only one life, 'twill soon be past,
> Only what's done for Christ will last.

III. The Responsibility of the Lad

"There is a lad here who has five barley loaves and two small fish" (6:9). The Lord Jesus would have never taken those loaves and fish from the boy's hand unless there had been a complete willingness on his part. Here was a youth who was involved in a situation of responsibility. When Andrew pointed him out, the lad knew that he could be of service and he wasn't slow to make that known. Responsibility has been defined as "our response to God's ability." Somehow this lad knew that in the hands of the Savior that little parcel of food could be sanctified and multiplied; so as soon as Andrew brought him to the Savior he acted with consummate responsibility.

A. The Lad Yielded His All to the Savior

"Jesus took the loaves, and when He had given thanks He distributed them to the disciples and the disciples to those sitting down; and likewise of the fish" (6:11). Notice that the loaves and the fish did not change or multiply at that particular moment. The emphasis here is on the willingness of Christ to accept the five loaves and two small fish.

What a glorious lesson this is for all who have eyes to see and ears to hear! Jesus Christ takes what we give to him. It does not matter how small our contribution might be: he takes what we have. Once the talents are in his hands he sanctifies them by the power of his cleansing life and love. We cannot read this story and have an excuse for holding back our five loaves and two small fish. We may sense our unworthiness and our utter sinfulness, but if we are prepared to yield our all to Jesus that is all that matters.

Illustration

At a meeting held near Oxford, England in connection with the building of a new church, a speaker made an eloquent appeal for funds, urging the audience to give all they had on them. All were impressed, and among them was a small boy who, when the offering was taken, placed a top and five marbles in the plate. In the vestry afterward one of the ushers was inclined to ridicule the boy's offering; but the chairman said, "I will give you twenty pounds for the top, and will take the marbles to Oxford, and will get five of my friends to give five pounds each for them." He wrote out his check for twenty pounds, and in due course forwarded the other twenty-five pounds. At the stonelaying, there was placed under the principal stone the top and five marbles from the little boy who gave all he had. So a little given for Jesus' sake will be made much by him.[2]

B. The Lad Trusted His All to the Savior

"And Jesus took the loaves, and when He had given thanks He distributed them to the disciples, and the disciples to those sitting down" (6:11). In the distribution the miracle took place. As he broke those loaves subtraction became multiplication; a lad's lunch became a meal for over five thousand men, women, and children (see Matt. 14:21). By his creative power, the Lord of all life compressed into a moment of time what takes months to happen naturally. This is what a miracle is all about. The important thing about this story is that the faith of the boy was involved in this miracle. It takes no imagination to realize that the boy was aware that the Savior was about to feed a multitude with his lunch; yet without hesitation he yielded his all and trusted his all to Christ. God honored that simple faith, and hungry people were fed to overflowing.

Illustration

A boy at school sensed the urge to start what he called "The Order of the Mustard Seed." He gathered a group of boys around him, and they began to pray that God would give them faith as a grain of mustard seed. That boy became Count Zinzendorf, and his little group was the beginning of what eventually became the Moravian movement which has pioneered missionary work worldwide. There was another little boy who gave his all to Jesus Christ while still on a farm, milking cows in the humblest of circumstances. God took that life and through it has reached more people than any other person in this generation. That little boy is the man we know today as evangelist Billy Graham.

Conclusion

We have seen what we mean by the gift of youth. All God wants is the availability, the potentiality, and the responsibility of an individual who is prepared to give his all. If we do our part God will do the rest, and the world will be blessed.

14

Youth Sunday: The Role of Youth
1 Timothy 4:10–16

"Let no one despise your youth, but be an example to the believers in word, in conduct, in love, in spirit, in faith, in purity" (4:12).

Introduction

For young people launching out upon life's responsibilities, Paul has an appropriate word to say in the passage before us. "Let no one despise your youth," exhorts the apostle, and then proceeds to show why the young are not to be despised: they have a role to play—something which each new generation needs to know.

When youthful achievements are remembered it is well to recall that Mozart was just seven when his first composition was published. Benjamin Franklin was a newspaper columnist at 16. At 22 Gladstone was a member of Parliament and at 24 Lord of the Treasury. William Pitt II was 24 when he became Prime Minister of Great Britain.

Washington was a distinguished colonel at 22. Napoleon commanded the army of France at 25. Before he was 17 Shelley was already an author and had translated half of Pliny's *Natural History*. John Calvin wrote his *Institutes of the Christian Religion* before he was 23. Spurgeon, the renowned Baptist preacher, was drawing the largest audiences of his generation before he was 21. How relevant, then, are Paul's words!

I. Youth Has Something to Offer

"Let no one despise your youth, but be an example to the believers in word, in conduct, in love, in spirit, in faith, in purity" (4:12). Paul was addressing these words to a young man who was about to assume pastoral responsibilities of the church in Ephesus, as well as other congregations in the areas surrounding that great metropolis. Because of his youth, Timothy stood in danger of being despised or looked down upon. Paul, therefore, exhorts him to be an example, a pattern, a model of the believers in a fivefold way:

A. The Example of Conversation

"Be an example . . . in word" (4:12). Timothy was to watch his speech life. He was to recognize that "death and life are in the power of the tongue" (Prov. 18:21). Like the psalmist, he was to pray this prayer daily, "Set a guard, O LORD, over my mouth. Keep watch over the door of my lips" (Ps. 141:3).

Never before has youth had so much to say as today. Thinking has been shaped in our homes, our churches, on our campuses, and in the country generally by the conversation of youth. There are many reasons for this. The mass media has made knowledge instantly available. Social pressures have also had a contribution; and the permissive climate of contemporary life has lifted the restrictions that once silenced our young people.

However it has come about, it is nonetheless an outstanding phenomenon of the day in which we live. Youth is speaking out. The question is, what are they saying? What effect will their words have upon the world they are shaping? That is where Christian youth has its golden opportunity. God has spoken his final word in Jesus Christ (see Heb. 1:1–2). It is the only word that can bring salvation, peace, and harmony to a sin-ridden world. That redemptive word can be relayed by young men and women who are prepared to be conversationalists for Jesus Christ. All life is shaped by words and our generation is no exception. What a responsibility rests upon the young to speak, and to speak well of Jesus Christ.

B. *The Example of Conduct*

"Be an example . . . in conduct" (4:12). Timothy was to remember that he was under the watchful eyes of young and old; therefore, his behavior had to be exemplary as befitted a man of God.

What a word this is for the young of our day! Youth makes an impact in our modern times by their behavior patterns, for example, the style of hair, dress code, music, speech, etc. Historians will someday record that this was the age when young people "did their thing." Here is where Christian youth can have its moment of destiny. Jesus Christ said that believers were to be as "the salt of the earth . . . [and] the light of the world" (Matt. 5:13–14). Salt arrests corruption, and light dispels darkness. This is what we are called to be in our homes, our churches, our offices, and in every area of national life. Conduct must never be neutral: it is either redemptive or destructive.

C. *The Example of Compassion*

"Be an example . . . in love" (4:12). This is the great word of the Bible—particularly in the New Testament. Such love comes only from heaven; it is the nature of

God, mediated through Jesus Christ, and imparted by the Holy Spirit. Timothy was to show this love to God, to his fellow Christians, and to non-believers.

We live in a world of lovelessness today. Hatred, racism, poverty, and bloodshed are all about us. There is only one cure for these evils: the love of God released in redemptive action. It is an interesting fact of history that all the major revivals that have swept churches, countries, and continents in the past have been channeled through young people. Joel prophesied this when he said that the Spirit of God would be poured out upon all flesh so that sons and daughters would prophesy, and young men would see visions (see Acts 2:16–17). Renewal comes through prophetic vision and action, and young people can make a difference in this area.

D. The Example of Confidence

"Be an example . . . in faith" (4:12). The faith spoken of here is trust in God. Timothy was to believe God, for "with God all things are possible" (Matt. 19:26). Here again is a word to our contemporary youth. In an age of skepticism and faithfulness we need to return to God, his Word, and his church. Without faith it is impossible to please God (see Heb. 11:6), to establish the home, the church, or the nation. Our whole democracy was founded on the God in whom we trust. We must recapture this faith by "looking unto Jesus, the author and finisher of our faith" (Heb. 12:2), and by hearing and obeying the Word of God, which is the channel of faith. Faith is the victory that overcomes the world (see 1 John 5:4). It is something to cherish and to share.

E. The Example of Chastity

"Be an example . . . in purity" (4:12). Timothy was to conduct himself in such a way that his character would be honorable before men and blameless before God. In an age of permissiveness and relativistic values, we need an army of young people who are going to reveal the character of God in terms of holy living. We need young men and women who can demonstrate that laughter can be holy, love can be holy, sex can be holy, pleasure can be holy, and business can be holy. While we are encouraged by youthful protests against pornography and other forms of immorality, we need still more examples of chastity and purity in our time.

II. Youth Has Something to Suffer

Paul reminds Timothy that "we both labor and suffer reproach, because we trust in the living God, who is the Savior of all men, especially of those who believe" (4:10). Timothy was to realize from the start that his trust in God was going to meet with opposition and rejection from many of his contemporaries. This is the way it has been throughout the centuries. No one can stand for the quality of life which youth has to offer without facing suffering and sacrifice.

A. There Is the Tyranny of Resistance

"We . . . labor . . . because we trust in the living God" (4:10). The word "labor" here means "toiling against odds," "working against opposition." Timothy was being warned that Christian living and witness would not always meet with public approval. He would face the tyranny of resistance from the world, the flesh, and the devil.

What was true in his day is just as true today. This is where we need the reality of Christian experience and the power of Jesus Christ in our lives. Let us not fool ourselves. Even in this day of so-called "tolerance" God is hated, Christ is hated, and the gospel is hated. The Bible says: "The natural man does not receive the things of the Spirit of God, for they are foolishness to him" (1 Cor. 2:14); and again: "The carnal mind is enmity against God; for it is not subject to the law of God, nor indeed can be" (Rom. 8:7). In fact, "friendship with the world is enmity with God. Whoever therefore wants to be a friend of the world makes himself an enemy of God" (James 4:4). To face this tyranny of resistance is a constant battle requiring not only the armor of God, but also the power of Christ. A dead fish will float with the current, but it takes a live one to swim against it. Are we prepared for the ministry of suffering? Remember the apostle said, "It has been granted on behalf of Christ, not only to believe in Him, but also to suffer for His sake" (Phil. 1:29).

B. There Is the Agony of Reproach

"We . . . suffer reproach, because we trust in the living God" (4:10). Timothy was called upon to face the fact that, like his Savior before him, he was to face shame, embarrassment, and reproach. This has been true throughout the history of the church. Sometimes it is open and brazen; other times it is silent and subtle—but just as hurtful. As we read the Gospels we note the jibes that were leveled at our Savior. People mocked him in that day and they mock him in ours, along with his followers. We have to be ready to face the agony of reproach. Thank God for those who will take a stand, who are prepared to endure the cross and despise the shame.

Illustration

Years ago a small group of Japanese believers were heckled and abused whenever they assembled to worship the Savior. But the persecutors could not shake the faith of the new converts. Each time the Christians gathered, the mob would throw stones at them, but they still faithfully continued to have their weekly meetings. Eventually the opposition became so great that the outdoor services had to be temporarily abandoned. Later, when a time of relative peace and tolerance had come to the community, many were won to Christ. Returning to the spot where the believers had frequently been attacked, they began to pick up some of the rocks. Using them as part of the building materials, they constructed a small house of worship, rejoicing that God had worked all things together for good. Jesus says that his followers will meet with suffering and heartache, but he admonishes them not to be discouraged. Earth's sorrows are meant to be stepping stones in the process of sanctification. Indeed, we "must through much tribulation enter into the kingdom of God" (Acts 14:22). Glorying in affliction will turn our troubles into spiritual triumphs![1]

III. Youth Has Something to Master

"Till I come, give attention to reading. . . . Do not neglect the gift that is in you. . . . Give yourself entirely" (4:13–15). If Timothy was going to prove that youth should not be despised, then he had to offer something, suffer something, but also master something. The passage before us suggests three areas that youth can master in order to find fulfillment in life:

A. There Is the Discipline of Time

"Give attention to reading, to exhortation, to doctrine" (4:13). Timothy was to give time to the public and private reading of Scripture, to the exhortation of his congregation, and to teaching. The application here is primarily pastoral, but the principles apply to all of Christian life. What he is saying is that we must give due attention to reading and to all that flows out of a life of study. Nothing is more tragic than to shrivel up in the areas of our thinking, reading, and studying. Indeed, the whole purpose of early education is that we might set the pattern for disciplined study for the rest of our lives. The Bible is true when it says, "As [a man] . . . thinks in his heart, so is he" (Prov. 23:7). We are only the measure of our capacity to think and to go on thinking. When this process dies we are no longer the people God intended us to be.

Illustration

Some years ago *Newsweek* printed a clever ad entitled *"Advice to a (Bored) Young Man."* It read as follows: Died, age 20; buried, age 60. The sad epitaph of too many Americans. Mummification sets in on too many young men at an age when they should be ripping the world wide open. For example: Many people reading this page are doing so with the aid of bifocals. Inventor? *B. Franklin*, age 79. The presses that printed this page were powered by electricity. One of the first harnessers? *B. Franklin*, age 40. Some are reading this on the campus of one of the Ivy League universities. Founder? *B. Franklin*, age 45. Others, in a library. Who founded the first library in America? *B. Franklin*, age 25. Some got their copy through the U.S. mail. Its father? *B. Franklin*, age 31. Now, think fire. Who started the first fire department, invented the lightning rod, designed a heating stove still in use today? *B. Franklin*, ages 31, 43, 36. Wit. Conversationalist. Economist. Philosopher. Diplomat. Favorite of the capitals of Europe. Journalist. Printer. Publisher. Linguist (spoke and wrote five languages). Advocate of paratroopers (from balloons) a century before the airplane was invented. All this until age 84. And he had exactly two years of formal schooling. It's a good bet that you already have more sheer knowledge than Franklin ever had when he was your age. Perhaps you think there's no use trying to think of anything new, that everything's been done. Wrong. The simple, agrarian America of Franklin's day didn't begin to need the answers we need today. *Go do something about it!* Tear out this page and read it on your 84th birthday. Ask yourself what took over in your life, indolence or ingenuity?[2]

B. There Is the Development of Gift

"Do not neglect the gift that is in you" (4:14). Undoubtedly, Paul is here referring to the one distinctive talent which was recognized by the leaders at the time of his ordination to the ministry, and the apostle was concerned lest Timothy might neglect this distinctive gift which God had given him to use in the ministry.

It is so easy for a minister or layman to lose the special abilities that God has given him by failure to exercise those powers in the cause of the gospel. Every person has a distinctive gift. There is something which God can do in us and through us that he cannot perform through anyone else. Therefore it is imperative that we develop that particular talent. To wrap it up in a sweat cloth and bury it in the ground is to merit our Lord's condemnation in the day of judgment. We must see, then, that we develop the powers that God has given us and then use them for his glory and the good of man.

C. There Is the Dedication of Life

"Meditate on these things; give yourself entirely to them, that your progress may be evident to all. Take heed to yourself" (4:15–16). Timothy was to think through all that Paul had said and then to dedicate himself not only to teaching, but to the one from whom such teaching had come, even the Lord Jesus Christ. Truth is only as sure as its source. Life is only as real as its source. Power is only as authentic as its source. When we dedicate ourselves we must think of the source of truth, of life, of power, and of all things good. Our commitment must be, first of all, to God, as revealed in Jesus Christ, and made real through the Holy Spirit. Youth cannot offer anything, suffer anything, or master anything without commitment to Christ.

Illustration

It is estimated there are some sixty thousand serious mountain climbers in the United States, and within that number a small elite group known as "hard men." For them, climbing mountains and scaling sheer rock faces is a part of their whole commitment to life. Their ultimate experience is called free soloing: climbing with no equipment and no safety ropes. John Baker is considered by many to be the best of the hard men. His skill has been acquired through commitment, dedication, and training. When he isn't climbing, he can be found in his California home hanging by his fingertips to strengthen his arms and hands. Where are the hard men and women for Jesus? Where are those who will bring all their energies to bear for the sake of Christ? That's the kind of people it is going to take to spread the gospel throughout the world in these closing years of the twentieth century.[3]

Conclusion

Jesus Christ is calling for young people who will face the challenge of their role in the contemporary life of today, who will be an example to their generation. The secret of such character and quality of living and serving is a personal relationship to the one who came, died, and rose again that we might have "life, and . . . have it more abundantly" (John 10:10). We must respond, as did the apostle Paul on the Damascus road, and say, "Lord, what do You want me to do?" (Acts 9:6)?

Endnotes

Chapter 1

1. *Sermons Illustrated* (Holland, Ohio, Mar. 17, 1987).
2. *Webster's New World Dictionary,* 1951.
3. R. V. G. Tasker, *Second Epistle of Paul to the Corinthians.* Tyndale New Testament Commentary (Grand Rapids; Eerdmans, 1958), p. 88.
4. V. Raymond Edman, *They Found the Secret* (Grand Rapids: Zondervan, 1960).
5. George V. McDaniel, *Proof,* quoted in Walter B. Knight, *Knight's Master Book of New Illustrations* (Grand Rapids: Eerdmans, 1956), p. 413.
6. J. D'Aubigne, quoted in *Choice Gleanings* (Grand Rapids: Gospel Folio Press, Nov. 1, 1979.)

Chapter 2

1. Dennis J. DeHaan, *Our Daily Bread* (Grand Rapids, Radio Bible Class, 1982).
2. Herbert Vander Lugt, *Our Daily Bread* (Grand Rapids, Radio Bible Class, 1982).

Chapter 3

1. Gordon MacDonald, *Ordering Your Private World* (Nashville: Nelson, 1985), p. 13.
2. Adapted and reprinted from *The Word for Every Day,* Alvin N. Rogness, copyright © Augsburg Publishing House, p. 108. Used by permission of Augsburg Fortress.
3. Homer A. Rodeheaver, copyright 1933 by Homer A. Rodeheaver. Renewed 1961 by The Rodeheaver Co.

Chapter 5

1. *Pulpit Helps*, (Chattanooga: AMG International).
2. Paul Rees, *World Vision Magazine* (April 1966).
3. B. Charles Hostetter, *Informer* (April 1961).

Chapter 6

1. *The Epistle*, quoted in *Pulpit Helps* (Chattanooga: AMG International, Dec. 1985), p. 6.
2. *Sermons Illustrated* (Holland, Ohio, Oct. 2, 1985).
3. *Free Will Baptist*, quoted in *Pulpit Helps* (Chattanooga: AMG International, April 1980).
4. *Tan Huma Rabbinic Literature*, quoted in *Sermons Illustrated* (Holland, Ohio, Nov. 22, 1986).
5. From *Scripture Union Songs and Choruses.*
6. *Choice Gleanings* (Grand Rapids: Gospel Folio Press, April 19, 1978).

Chapter 7

1. From *The Keswick Hymnbook*. Used by permission of Marshall-Pickering.

Chapter 8

1. From the book *The Charles L. Allen Treasury* by Charles L. Wallis, ed., copyright © 1970 by Fleming H. Revell Company, p. 88. Used by permission of Fleming H. Revell Company.
2. Henry G. Bosch, *Our Daily Bread* (Grand Rapids: Gospel Folio Press, 1975).
3. Stanley C. Baldwin, *How to Build Your Christian Character* (Wheaton, Ill: Victor Books, 1982), p. 118, adapted by permission.

Chapter 9

1. *Crossroads*, quoted in *Pulpit Helps* (Chattanooga: AMG International, Sept. 1984).
2. *Our Daily Bread* (Grand Rapids: Radio Bible Class, n.d.).
3. *Christian Digest*, quoted in Walter B. Knight, *Knight's Master Book of New Illustrations* (Grand Rapids: Eerdmans, 1956), p. 406.
4. Nelson Bitton, *The Regeneration of China*, quoted in ibid., p. 99.
5. *Boy's World*, quoted in Paul Lee Tan, *Encyclopedia of 7,700 Illustrations* (Dallas: Bible Communications, 1979), pp. 514–15.

Endnotes

6. James Montgomery Boice, *The Sermon on the Mount* (Grand Rapids: Zondervan, 1972), p. 218.

Chapter 10

1. Ian Macpherson, "You Cannot Better the Body," in *Prophetic Witness*. Vol. 7, no. 9. (Loughborough, England: Prophetic Witness Movement International, Sept. 1983), p. 13.

Chapter 11

1. M. R. De Haan, *Our Daily Bread* (Grand Rapids: Radio Bible Class, June 2, 1960).

Chapter 12

1. Ray O. Jones, quoted in Paul Lee Tan, *Encyclopedia of 7,700 Illustrations*. (Dallas: Bible Communications, 1979), p. 1184.
2. *Our Daily Bread* (Grand Rapids: Radio Bible Class, n.d.).
3. *Sermons Illustrated* (Holland, Ohio, June 12, 1986).
4. *Sermons Illustrated* (Holland, Ohio, May 3, 1986).

Chapter 13

1. *Sermons Illustrated* (Holland, Ohio, Dec. 19, 1986).
2. *The Family Herald and Weekly Star*, quoted in Walter B. Knight, *3,000 Illustrations for Christian Service* (Grand Rapids: Eerdmans, 1952), p. 305.

Chapter 14

1. *Sermons Illustrated* (Holland, Ohio, Mar. 3, 1986).
2. *Newsweek, Inc.* Copyright 1967. Used by permission.
3. *Sermons Illustrated* (Holland, Ohio, Sept. 11, 1987).

For Further Reading

Part 1: Annual Occasions

Baron, David. *The Visions and Prophecies of Zechariah.* Fincastle, Va.: Scripture Truth Book Co., 1962.

Collins, G. M. M. *The New Bible Commentary* (Zechariah). Ed. F. Davidson, A. M. Stibbs, and E. F. Kevan. Downers Grove, Ill.: InterVarsity Press, 1953.

Dodds, Marcus. *The Vision of a Prophet.* London: Hodder & Stoughton.

Ellicott, Charles J. *Commentary on the Whole Bible,* vol. 5. Grand Rapids: Zondervan Publishing House, 1954.

Feinburg, Charles L. *God Remembers.* 1950. Reprint. Portland: Multnomah Press, 1977.

Laney, J. Carl. *Everyman's Bible Commentary.* (Zechariah). Chicago: Moody Press, 1984.

Meyer, F. B. *The Prophet of Hope: Studies in Zechariah.* London: Marshall, Morgan & Scott, 1952.

Moore, T. V. *A Commentary on Zechariah.* Carlisle, Pa.: Banner of Truth Trust, 1958.

Tatford, Frederick A. *The Prophet of the Myrtle Grove: An Exposition of the Prophecy of Zechariah.* Worthing, England: Henry E. Walter, Ltd., 1971.

Unger, Merrill F. *Zechariah: Prophet of Messiah's Glory.* Grand Rapids: Zondervan Publishing House, 1963.

Part 2: Special Occasions

Bodey, Richard Allen. *Good News for All Seasons: Twenty-Six Sermons for Special Days.* Grand Rapids: Baker Book House, 1987.

Ford, W. Herschel. *Simple Sermons for Special Days and Occasions.* Grand Rapids: Baker Book House, 1985.

Baptism Service

Carson, Alexander. *Baptism, Its Mode and Its Subjects.* 1957. Reprint, Grand Rapids: Kregel Publications, 1981.

Gilmore, Alec, ed. *Christian Baptism.* London: Lutterworth Press, 1960.

Howard, James Keir. *New Testament Baptism.* London: Pickering & Inglis, 1970.

Warns, Johannes. *Baptism: Studies in the Original Christian Baptism, Its History and Conflicts.* Minneapolis: Klock and Klock Christian Publishers, 1980.

Watson, T. E. *Baptism Not for Infants.* Ribchester, Lancs., England: 1962.

Missions Sunday

Beals, Paul A. *A People for His Name: A Church-Based Missions Strategy.* Pasadena, Calif.: William Carey Library, 1985.

Conn, Harvie M. *Eternal Word and Changing Worlds: Theology, Anthropology, and Mission in Trialogue.* Grand Rapids: Zondervan Publishing House, 1984.

Cook, Harold R. *Introduction to Christian Missions.* Rev. ed. Chicago: Moody Press, 1971.

Culver, Robert Duncan. *A Greater Commission: A Theology of World Missions.* Chicago: Moody Press, 1984.

Duncan, Homer. *Divine Intent.* 3d rev. ed. Lubbock, Tex.: World-wide Missionary Crusader, 1982.

Elliot, James. *The Journal of Jim Elliot.* Ed. Elisabeth Elliot. Old Tappan, N.J.: Fleming H. Revell, 1978.

Hesselgrave, David John, ed. *Planting Churches Cross-Culturally: A Guide for Home and Foreign Missions.* Grand Rapids: Baker Book House, 1980.

Kane, J. Herbert. *Christian Missions in Biblical Perspective.* Grand Rapids: Baker Book House, 1976.

———. *The Christian World Mission: Today and Tomorrow.* Grand Rapids: Baker Book House, 1981.

———. *A Concise History of Christian World Mission: A Panoramic View of Missions from Pentecost to the Present.* Grand Rapids: Baker Book House, 1978.

———. *A Global View of Christian Missions: From Pentecost to the Present.* Grand Rapids: Baker Book House, 1971.

———. *Understanding Christian Missions.* Grand Rapids: Baker Book House, 1974.

Peters, George William. *A Biblical Theology of Missions.* Chicago: Moody Press, 1973.

Stott, John R. W. *Christian Mission in the Modern World.* Downers Grove, Ill.: InterVarsity Press, 1975.

Youth Sunday

Benson, Warren S., and Mark H. Senter III. *Complete Book of Youth Ministry.* Chicago: Moody Press, 1987.

Campbell, Ross. *How to Really Love Your Teenager.* Wheaton, Ill.: Victor Books, 1981.

Campolo, Tony. *You Can Make a Difference.* Waco, Tex.: Word, Inc., 1984.

Cook, Robert. *It's Tough to Be a Teenager.* Wheaton: Scripture Press, 1955.

Dobson, James C., Jr. *Preparing for Adolescence.* Santa Ana, Calif.: Vision House Publishers, 1978.

―――. *The Strong-Willed Child: Birth Through Adolescence.* Wheaton, Ill.: Tyndale House Publishers, 1978.

Duvall, Evelyn Ruth (Millis). *Parents and Teenager: Living and Loving.* Nashville: Broadman Press, 1976.

Eble, Diane. *Personal Best.* Grand Rapids: Zondervan Publishing House, 1991.

Eble, Diane, Chris Lutes, and Kris Bearss. *Welcome to High School.* Grand Rapids: Zondervan Publishing House, 1991.

Fleischmann, Paul, ed. *Discipling the Young Person.* San Bernardino, Calif.: Here's Life Publishers, Inc., 1985.

Getz, Gene A. *The Measure of a Family.* Glendale, Calif.: Regal Books, 1976.

Johnston, Jerry J. *The Edge of Evil.* Waco, Tex.: Word Publishing, 1989.

Kesler, Jay, and Ronald A. Beers. *Parents and Teenagers.* Wheaton, Ill.: Victor Books, 1984.

McDowell, Josh and Bill Jones. *The Teenage Q & A Book.* Dallas: Word Publishing, 1990.

Overton, Grace Sloan. *Living with Parents.* Nashville: Broadman Press, 1954.

Richards, Lawrence O. *Youth Ministry: Its Renewal in the Local Church.* Rev. ed. Grand Rapids: Zondervan Publishing House, 1985.

Stevens, Douglas. *Called to Care: Youth Ministry for the Church.* Grand Rapids: Zondervan Publishing House, 1985.

Wiersbe, Warren W. *Be Challenged! Profiles of Six Bible Teenagers.* Chicago: Moody Press, 1971. Rev. ed. 1982.